RAND SOCIAL AND ECONOMIC WELL-BEING

Algorithmic Equity

A Framework for Social Applications

Osonde A. Osoba, Benjamin Boudreaux, Jessica Saunders,
J. Luke Irwin, Pam A. Mueller, Samantha Cherney

For more information on this publication, visit www.rand.org/t/RR2708

Library of Congress Cataloging-in-Publication Data is available for this publication.
ISBN: 978-1-9774-0313-1

Published by the RAND Corporation, Santa Monica, Calif.

© Copyright 2019 RAND Corporation

RAND® is a registered trademark.

www.rand.org

Preface

This report is an examination of potential decisionmaking pathologies in social institutions that increasingly leverage algorithms. We frame social institutions as operating as collections of *decision pipelines* in which algorithms can increasingly feature either as decision aids or decisionmakers. Then we examine how different perspectives on equity or fairness inform the use of algorithms in the context of three sample institutions: auto insurance, recruitment, and criminal justice. We then highlight challenges and recommendations to improve equity in the use of algorithms for institutional decisionmaking.

This report is funded by RAND internal funds. The goal is to inform decisionmakers and regulators grappling with equity considerations in the deployment of algorithmic decision aids, particularly in public institutions. We hope our report can also serve to inform private-sector decisionmakers and the lay public.

Community Health and Environmental Policy Program

RAND Social and Economic Well-Being is a division of the RAND Corporation that seeks to actively improve the health and social and economic well-being of populations and communities throughout the world. This research was conducted in the Community Health and Environmental Policy Program within RAND Social and Economic Well-Being. The program focuses on such topics as infrastructure, science and technology, community design, community health promotion, migration and population dynamics, transportation, energy, and climate and the environment, as well as other policy concerns that are influenced by the natural and built environment, technology, and community organizations and institutions that affect well-being. For more information, email chep@rand.org.

RAND Ventures

The RAND Corporation is a research organization that develops solutions to public policy challenges to help make communities throughout the world safer and more secure, healthier and more prosperous. RAND is nonprofit, nonpartisan, and committed to the public interest.

RAND Ventures is a vehicle for investing in policy solutions. Philanthropic contributions support our ability to take the long view, tackle tough and often-controversial topics, and share our findings in innovative and compelling ways. RAND's research findings and recommendations are based on data and evidence, and therefore do not necessarily reflect the policy preferences or interests of its clients, donors, or supporters.

Funding for this venture was provided by gifts from RAND supporters and income from operations.

Contents

Preface iii

Figures and Tables vii

Summary ix

Abbreviations xi

CHAPTER ONE

Introduction 1

The Rise of Algorithmic Decisionmaking 2

Identifying and Scoping the Research Questions 4

Approach and Methods 4

Organization of This Report 5

CHAPTER TWO

Concepts of Equity 7

Perspectives on Equity 8

Equity in Practice: Impossibilities and Trade-Offs 15

Competing Concepts of Equity: The Case of COMPAS 17

Metaethical Aspects of Algorithmic Equity 21

CHAPTER THREE

Domain Exploration: Algorithms in Auto Insurance 23

The Auto Insurance Decision Pipeline 25

Relevant Concepts of Equity in Auto Insurance 28

Equity Challenges 30

Closing Thoughts 31

CHAPTER FOUR

Domain Exploration: Algorithms in Employee Recruitment 33

Relevant Concepts of Equity in Employment 34

Benefits of Recruitment Algorithms 36

Employment Algorithm Decision Pipeline 36

Equity Challenges in Recruitment Algorithms..39
Closing Thoughts 42

CHAPTER FIVE
Domain Exploration: Algorithms in U.S. Criminal Justice Systems 45
The Criminal Justice Decision Pipeline 46
Relevant Concepts of Equity in Criminal Justice... 48
Equity Challenges...49
Closing Thoughts 51

CHAPTER SIX
Analytic Case Study: Auditing Algorithm Use in North Carolina's Criminal
      Justice System 53
Background...53
Assessment of Algorithmic Bias 56
Summary of Audit Analysis..59

CHAPTER SEVEN
Insights and Recommendations...61
Insights from Domain Explorations 61
Recommendations and Useful Frameworks 65
Closing Remarks 73

APPENDIX
A. Supplemental Tables..75

References 77

Figures and Tables

Figures

3.1.	State Auto Insurance Regulatory Regimes.	26
3.2.	Notional Rendition of the Auto Insurance Decision Pipeline.	27
4.1.	Notional Rendition of Decision Pipeline for Employment and Recruiting	37
5.1.	Notional Rendition of Decision Pipeline for the U.S. Criminal Justice System	45

Tables

2.1.	Summary of the Simpler Statistical Concepts of Equity	12
6.1.	Relationship Between Supervision Levels and Risk/Needs Levels	55
6.2.	Supervision Level Minimum Contact Standards	55
6.3.	Distribution of Probation Assessment Results by Race	57
6.4.	One-Year Violation Rates by Race and by Supervision Level	57
6.5.	Summary of Multivariate Logistic Regression Results—Odds Ratio	58
7.1.	Notional Basic Checklist for Algorithmic Equity	70
7.2.	A Range of Governance Options for Algorithms	73

Summary

This report examines the question of *fairness*, or *equity*, in the context of social institutions. The aim is to guide the equitable use of algorithmic decisionmaking tools in social applications. (We define *algorithms* as advanced decisionmaking or decision support artifacts that exhibit "intelligent behavior.") In this report, RAND researchers use a case-study–based methodology to provide a better understanding of key issues related to algorithmic equity that recur across applications.

We begin this report by framing the concept of *equity*, deriving our definition from the disparate traditions in which equity is typically studied: law, philosophy, and—now—statistical machine learning. Three problems occur with any attempt to conceptualize equity. First, equity is not a singular concept. Different equity norms often apply to any given social institution. Second, seemingly reasonable concepts of equity may be contested or even incompatible with each other. Third, prescriptive and theoretical concepts of equity sometimes differ from common practical concepts. These problems can give rise to *equity challenges*—contested deviations from the principles, rules, and values inherent within institutions. We highlight the practical impact of some of these problems through an examination of the debate surrounding the Correctional Offender Management Profiling for Alternative Sanctions (COMPAS) criminal risk-assessment algorithm. Our examination underscores the importance of contextual, case-driven exploration of algorithmic equity.

We then explore three domains in which algorithmic decisionmaking devices are increasingly used: auto insurance pricing, employment recruitment, and criminal justice. We frame each domain as a *decision pipeline*, in which algorithms can feature as key decisionmaking tools at different points in the pipeline. We identify challenges related to algorithms' equitable use in these decision pipelines. Our explorations are meant to be illustrative, not exhaustive, and are not meant to be complete depictions of the sociotechnical systems under discussion.

In the auto insurance domain, the most common operative concept of equity focuses on individual risk fairness. In other words, individuals expect a rate commensurate to their insurance risk or expected cost to the company. Social adequacy norms, such as affordability and the nonuse of sensitive attributes, modulate this basic equity norm. The key algorithmic equity challenges are (1) *redlining*, in which risk premiums deviate from individual risk fairness on the basis of geographic location, and (2) algorithms enabling the indirect violation of regulatory norms that ban the use of sensitive attributes to determine risk premiums.

In the employee recruitment domain, the key equity norms are *disparate treatment* and *disparate impact*, both of which feature in federal U.S. employment law. U.S. law forbids the disparate treatment of job seekers based on sensitive attributes. The law also prohibits the use of irrelevant recruitment practices that disparately impact *protected classes* (characteristics of individuals that are formally barred from use in decisionmaking). We highlight three key algorithmic equity challenges in algorithmic recruitment: (1) the lack of representativeness of available training data, (2) the imperfect and incomplete nature of *ground truth* (measurable facts that an algorithmic system is optimized to predict) data about job merit, and (3) the use of algorithms to avoid regulatory accountability. These are just a few of the equity challenges faced by algorithm use in employee recruitment.

In the criminal justice domain, two key equity norms are *equal protection* (or equal treatment) and *due process*. Due process refers to fairness in the relationship between an individual and the state—in this case, the provision of notice and the opportunity for a hearing. These norms provide a common basis for algorithmic equity challenges. Algorithmic models can be hard to certify for equal treatment, especially given the prevalence of *proxy variables* (variables closely correlated with or predictive of variables of interests) for attributes that would typically be subject to heightened review, otherwise known as *strict scrutiny*. Current applications of algorithms in the justice system influence outcomes without giving notice to affected individuals. The opacity of the algorithms also challenges due process. We augment this discussion with the results of an analytic audit of an algorithmic risk assessment tool in the North Carolina criminal justice system. We find that this tool performs quite well on different dimensions of equity, but questions still exist about how implementation practices produce unfair outcomes.

From a regulatory perspective, hiding data about sensitive attributes from algorithms to ensure fair outcomes is no longer a viable strategy, as algorithmic models are now adept at finding probabilistic proxies for protected class membership. This suggests that regulatory mechanisms that try to assure equity by barring specific types of model inputs need to be reviewed. We also highlight the need for clarity on domain-specific concepts of equity, as well as the importance of different forms of algorithmic transparency. Implementation practices, in the application context external to the algorithms, also affect the equity of an institution.

We end with a discussion of recommendations and interventions that can foster more equitable use of algorithms. These include *bottom-up mechanisms* (e.g., checklists, auditing frameworks) and *top-down mechanisms* (e.g., governance, regulatory, or voluntary compliance mechanisms).

Abbreviations

AI	artificial intelligence
CF	counterfactual fairness
COMPAS	Correctional Offender Management Profiling for Alternative Sanctions
DP	demographic parity
EEOC	Equal Employment Opportunity Commission
EO	equal opportunity
EU	European Union
FTU	fairness through unawareness
GDPR	General Data Protection Regulation
IF	individual fairness

CHAPTER ONE

Introduction

Social institutions—markets, social media platforms, criminal justice systems, and employment sectors—increasingly leverage algorithms for decisionmaking purposes. Although these social institutions may seem quite different, we can visualize all of them as operating as collections of *decision pipelines* that "distribute [rights] and duties" to participants and "determine the division of advantages" from social interactions according to established rules (Rawls, 2009, p. 7).

At its core, this report is an examination of pathologies in social institutions' use of algorithmic decisionmaking processes. The primary focus of our discussion is to understand how to think about and evaluate the *equitable* use of algorithms in decisionmaking systems across a range of specific applications.

Agents—individual people or meaningful aggregates thereof—within institutions have expectations of how the institution operates and how people are fairly treated within these institutions. These expectations may be explicitly codified (through laws, regulations, and contracts) or implicitly defined (through incomplete contracts and social interaction). Things go awry when the process or outcomes of decisions diverge from the legitimate institutional expectations of stakeholders. For example, this occurs when similarly entitled people are treated differently in a criminal justice proceeding or employment decision, or when some forms of speech are arbitrarily censored. We use the term *equity challenges* to refer to these deviations from inherent institutional values that affect the fair treatment of stakeholders.

Unaddressed equity challenges can undermine the stability and legitimacy of social institutions and can have severe ramifications for affected persons. Examples of unaddressed institutional equity challenges include the grievances underlying many historical movements, such as the restriction of royal power through the Magna Carta, the suffragette movement, the quest for civil rights, and today's Black Lives Matter. Arguably, a significant part of the history of law and social reform deals with the adaptation of institutions and mechanisms to address equity challenges.

The Rise of Algorithmic Decisionmaking

The advent of *algorithmic systems* in the 20th century adds a new dimension to achieving equity in social institutions. We use the term *algorithmic systems*, or *algorithms*, to refer to advanced decisionmaking or decision-support artifacts that exhibit "intelligent behavior" (Nilsson, 1998). The myriad implementations of artificial intelligence (AI) are examples of such artifacts.[1] This includes machine learning models, which are often trained on available data. Algorithmic systems have progressed in ability through improvements in computing technology and the availability of massive data sets for training. Advanced AI systems now perform as well as humans (and sometimes better) in some narrow intelligence tasks (Taigman et al., 2014).

These high-performance algorithms promise a form of objectivity. They are thought to provide a path toward consistent decisionmaking. They are tools for better applying available information to make real-world decisions with less noise or variance and without the influence of human subjectivities, emotions, and prejudices. Algorithm use can also increase the speed, efficiency, and accuracy of decisionmaking. These reasons help explain why algorithmic systems are a growing part of institutional decisionmaking, either by providing support for human decisionmakers or by making decisions autonomously.

However, the (often) data-driven nature of these algorithms means that the algorithmic promise of objectivity is better described as a promise of *consistency*—and consistency does not mean infallibility or the absence of bias (Osoba and Welser, 2017a; Barocas and Selbst, 2016; Hadfield-Menell et al., 2016). Algorithmic systems do not necessarily align with institutional values, such as equity, even if they exhibit highly intelligent behavior.[2] This *value alignment* problem has deeper implications when misaligned algorithmic systems are deployed in high-stakes applications that have significant impact on people's lives (Arnold, Kasenberg, and Scheutz, 2017).

Many algorithmic systems learn by optimizing for accuracy. This *ground truth* accuracy criterion is often taken at face value as the most important standard for assessment to the near-exclusion of other relevant normative criteria (Soares and Fallenstein, 2014). It is often easier to articulate an accuracy evaluation criterion in mathematical form. For example, we evaluate an image classification model using an easy-to-calculate out-of-sample accuracy statistic: the misclassification rate. This is the rate at which the model fails at the classification task. Some implementations of supervised classifica-

---

[1]   AI tends to be difficult to define. In this report, we define it as artificial means for making decisions or otherwise achieving goals in the world. We augment this definition in Osoba and Welser, 2017b. Most current models of AI rely on improvements in the practice (and sometimes, in the theory) of statistical machine learning.

[2]   Another example of misalignment is the use of inscrutable decisionmaking tools for applications that should prioritize transparency and procedural justice.

tion models will learn by optimizing this statistic directly. Statistical machine learning models all feature a similar evaluation criterion framing.[3]

Well-trained algorithmic models can often perform at superhuman accuracy levels when the evaluation criterion is so well defined. There are numerous examples of this level of accuracy, such as in image recognition, speech recognition, lip reading, and medical image analysis. The utility and relative performance of these models drives their adoption in other domains, such as criminal justice, employment recruitment, and even journalism.

As algorithmic systems are adopted more widely in decisionmaking in social applications, an additional level of complexity develops. Although algorithms are mathematically precise, the norms that govern these algorithms are often contested or ambiguous, and even unanimously chosen norms may not be reducible to mathematical principles (we explore this ambiguity and mathematical irreducibility point in more detail in the next chapter). Algorithms are also susceptible to *reward hacking*, in which algorithms working toward a seemingly specified norm can create unintended or unexpected consequences (Amodei et al., 2016).[4]

Equity challenges represent a specific form of value misalignment. Concrete examples of equity challenges specifically caused by the use of algorithmic systems include

- racial differences in the error rates of recidivism risk estimation models (Angwin et al., 2016)
- gender differences in accuracy of facial recognition systems used for surveillance (Buolamwini and Gebru, 2018)
- race-correlated differences in exposure to algorithmic defamation (Sweeney, 2013)
- unequal distribution of public services (O'Leary, 2013).

A higher-level systemic concern is that of *automation bias*, in which investing algorithms with decisionmaking responsibility can foster an uncritical reliance on algorithmic decision products (Osoba and Welser, 2017b). This risk underscores the importance of broader institutional dynamics and the role for clear guidelines and processes for how institutions use algorithms.

---

[3]   Most machine learning models fall into one of three categories: supervised, unsupervised, and reinforcement learning. Each works by evaluating an accuracy criterion directly or indirectly. Supervised machine learning models learn by minimizing an estimate of a *loss function* that encodes the accuracy criterion for the learning task. Unsupervised machine learning models often learn by optimizing a *goodness-of-fit criterion* that encodes how much the model explains observed data samples. Reinforcement learning models learn by maximizing a *reward function*—a measure of how much reward the model can extract from the environment.

[4]   An example is a hypothetical mopping robot that makes its own messes to seem like it is doing more work and gain a reward (Storm, 2016).

Identifying and Scoping the Research Questions

The relative novelty of algorithmic systems means there are currently few robust and tested institutional responses for addressing equity challenges introduced by these systems. Furthermore, it is unclear how to adapt preexisting legal and political mechanisms for addressing standard equity challenges to algorithms.

We aim to help address this need in this report. The goal of this report is to develop frameworks for *recognizing*, *adjudicating*, and *redressing* equity challenges that arise specifically due to the use of algorithmic systems. We examine the following questions:

- What do algorithmic equity challenges look like in different applications?
- What are the criteria for assessing algorithmic equity challenges?
- What mechanisms exist for correcting sustained algorithmic equity challenges, and how do existing legal and social norms apply?
- Are new mechanisms or other responses necessary?

Approach and Methods

To address these questions, we develop a framework for examining algorithmic decisionmaking and work through three domain explorations. This method is consistent with recently developed approaches for analyzing ethical issues in technology development practice (Vallor, Green, and Raicu, 2018).

Identifying a universal prescriptive formalization for algorithmic equity is infeasible. Our goal is to develop a richer understanding of algorithmic equity concerns at a higher level than just a single context. We use a case-based approach to understanding algorithmic equity by examining three social institutions in which algorithms are being used to inform or make decisions:

- automobile insurance markets
- job recruitment practices
- the criminal justice system.

These institutions use algorithms for different purposes and thus provide a broad range of examples to assess algorithmic equity.

We conceptualize these institutions as decision pipelines, with algorithms featuring at some decision points in each pipeline. We then examine questions of equity for specific algorithmic decision points in each institution—e.g., rate-setting in auto insurance, resume screening in recruitment, and recidivism risk estimation in the criminal justice system. As a final step, we use our explorations of equity in each of these domains to identify cross-cutting concerns and inform general principles identifying, adjudicating, and redressing algorithmic equity challenges.

Our discussion draws mainly on the following sources:

- peer-reviewed literature on computer science, economics, philosophy, and law
- case law at the federal (and occasionally the state) level
- consultations with domain experts
- documented industry standards of practice
- relevant popular reports or discussions.

Organization of This Report

In Chapter Two, we discuss concepts of equity from philosophical, legal, and technical standpoints to draw insights that apply across algorithmic decisionmaking contexts. Chapters Three, Four, and Five are explorations of the use of algorithms in insurance, employment applications, and criminal justice, respectively. Chapter Six contains a deep dive into an algorithm audit of the North Carolina criminal justice system. Finally, Chapter Seven offers overall insights and practical policy recommendations for governance and institutional mechanisms.

CHAPTER TWO

Concepts of Equity

The focus on algorithmic equity immediately raises certain questions. What is equity, or fairness?[1] What are the relevant concepts of equity or fairness for assessing specific social institutions? And how do we validate equity in an algorithmic decisionmaking context?

Equity is a property of a decisionmaking agent or institution. An institution is fair because of a quality of its decisionmaking process (*procedural equity*) and/or because of a quality of the outcomes of its decisionmaking (*outcome equity*). The nature of that property of equity is both context-dependent and deeply contested, especially in discussions of equity in social and policy applications (Young, 1995; Moulin, 2004; Binns, 2018). Most people in modern American life have strong beliefs about the nature of equity in social institutions, even if these beliefs are incomplete or not explicitly spelled out. Later, we discuss the example of the Correctional Offender Management Profiling for Alternative Sanctions (COMPAS) recidivism risk assessment algorithm to demonstrate how competing approaches to equity manifest in part based on one's societal standpoint.

Many questions of equity admit framing as an *allocative*, or distributive, concern: How do we allocate *rights* or *burdens* subject to the different legitimate *claims* of stakeholders (Young, 1995; Moulin, 2004)?[2] Rights are broadly construed to include rights to goods, service, or processes. The right to a vote is a concrete example. Burdens are similarly broadly construed as assignments of obligations. Concrete examples include mandatory military service or even the burden of elevated risk of privacy breach. A legitimate claim here would be a normatively justified assertion or assignment of desert.

---

[1] Our use of the terms *equity* and *fairness* are interchangeable, but we default to using the term equity to avoid the intuitive association that fairness has with "equal treatment" standards. Equal treatment in the sense of consistency across cases is often not the controlling equity standard for a social application (as we argue later in this report). We discuss a variety of other closely related terms (e.g., *equality, nondiscrimination, bias-free*), but we do not attempt a systematic analysis of the relation between these concepts.

[2] Many algorithmic equity concerns can be further construed as problems of allocation under resource constraints. For example, Alice and Bob each want to withdraw $5, but the bank only has $9 on hand. Alice and Bob both have legitimate *claims* (i.e., accepted or uncontested assertions of ownership), but both claims cannot be satisfied. How does the algorithm determine which person gets his or her money?

The legitimacy of claims and the factors that determine claims (the claimant's *type, fitness,* or *entitlement*) are the subject of context-specific principles and/or precedent. The type of a claimant is a complete description of the claimant for the purposes of the allocation decision. It determines and limits an individual's entitlement to the decision outcomes (Young, 1995). An example of a claim type would be the democratic principle of "one citizen, one vote," which gives each citizen a legitimate claim to an equal right to vote. Our discussion will proceed under the assumption that the nature of underlying claims can be discoverable in context, although we recognize that it will rarely be obvious.

Allocative equity—the proper distribution of rights and burdens—is a natural frame for a policy-focused discussion of algorithmic equity in decisionmaking processes. A separate frame is that of *representational equity*, which concerns the long-term fair representation of persons throughout society.[3] The line between allocative and representational equity can be blurry. Significant inequalities in income or high-status positions can lead to representational harms to those not represented in those groups. On the other hand, representational inequity might have implications for allocational equity—for instance, unequal representation could discourage a nonrepresented person from participation in a social institution. This report focuses primarily on allocative equity: the allocations or assignments of such rights or burdens as jobs, surveillance attention, and risk premiums. However, representational equity issues also play a part, especially in our discussion of employment.

Perspectives on Equity

The question of equity is an ancient one, with roots at least as far back as the Talmud, Plato's *Republic*, and Book V of Aristotle's *Nicomachean Ethics*.[4] A detailed exploration of historic concepts of equity may even yield other, older expositions.[5] Debates over such concepts of equity have proceeded for millennia—a point which underscores that there is no single consensus view, nor is there likely to be a fully satisfying overarching theory in the near term.

In this report, we highlight more-recent framings of equity from the philosophical, the legal, and the mathematical-statistical perspectives. These perspectives inform

---

[3]   We take the distinction between allocative and representational equity from Crawford, 2017. However, we have not followed her full definitions of these concepts.

[4]   Aristotle recommends an allocation rule called the "principle of proportionality." The Talmud recommends an allocation rule now called the "contested garment rule." Both yield different outcomes (except when the competing claims are exactly equal). This furnishes our first example of contestation in equity principles. We highlight a more recent example in our discussion of the COMPAS recidivism risk prediction tool.

[5]   An exhaustive historical exploration lies well outside the scope of this report.

U.S. laws and governance, provide a set of concepts that are familiar to many stakeholders, and offer insight into an assessment of algorithmic equity.

We do not argue for any specific approach in this report but aim to point out the plurality of views. As much as possible, we evaluate equity claims from within the norms of existing social institutions rather than from an abstract philosophical perspective.

Philosophical Concepts of Equity

The philosophical tradition has attempted to systematically explain, justify, and shape our everyday intuitions and more-considered judgments about what constitutes equity or fairness in social institutions. As there is an almost-infinite literature on these issues, we provide a short description of several important perspectives.[6]

Egalitarianism

Egalitarian approaches hold that social institutions must reflect the fundamental moral equality of persons. Of course, there are disagreements in the literature about what it means for persons to be equal and how this needs to be manifested in social institutions.

John Rawls offers an influential view that just institutions are guided by principles that individuals would choose from an "original position" of fairness. According to Rawls, many of the factors that have historically determined our allotment of resources—such as race or gender—are "arbitrary from a moral point of view" (Rawls, 2009, p. 72). The fair principles of justice are chosen from behind a hypothetical "veil of ignorance" that hides these morally arbitrary factors. Rawls argues that persons in a fair position behind this veil of ignorance would choose, very roughly, a principle of equal basic rights and a distributive principle that maximizes the resources of the least well-off members of society. The subtleties regarding the setup of the original position and the ultimate choice of principles of justice are out of scope here, but the key concept for our purposes is an account of justice that is based on a fair decisionmaking process, and one that has ramifications for just allocative outcomes. An extension of this view to algorithmic decisionmaking might suggest that algorithms should also operate behind a veil of ignorance without considering factors associated with race, gender, or other morally arbitrary features.[7]

An alternative egalitarian view, sometimes described as *luck-egalitarianism*, builds off of Rawls' insight that certain factors outside of a person's control—again, such factors as race, gender, or even inherited social status—should not determine distributive

---

[6]   We have selected philosophical approaches primarily from the Western tradition because these seem to be the approaches that have most informed legal and technical concepts within Western institutions; of course, many non-Western perspectives inform equity discussions as well.

[7]   We do not presume that Rawls himself holds this view, as his focus is on the basic structure of society, rather than specific institutional decisionmaking.

outcomes.[8] These views hold that distributions of resources are equitable when they reflect the free choices of persons; for example, a person has a free choice to study hard for an academic test that influences college admission, but cannot choose to be born into a rich family. Luck-egalitarians might argue that algorithms perpetuate and contribute to inequity when they reflect historical inequalities based on unchosen factors, such as gender, race, or social class. On the other hand, algorithms that accurately reflect the effects of the choices of affected persons, such as a person's decision to drive drunk, promote fairer outcomes.

Relational egalitarian views focus less on distributive outcomes and more on the institutional factors that enable persons to act in society as equals. Although resources are important to achieving this ideal, the emphasis of relational egalitarians is rather to end socially imposed oppression (Anderson, 1999), to ensure the equal status and rank of all persons in society (Scheffler, 2012), or to provide the basic conditions for equal democratic participation (Walzer, 1983). Social institutions' algorithms might work toward this goal, as they can be consistently applied and cannot be directly affected by social status or rank as a human would be. However, even consistent application of an algorithm might reflect and contribute to existing forms of social oppression, inequality of status, or political marginalization. An example of the latter is the case of the Street Bump application, in which the city of Boston used smartphones to detect the presence of potholes and report them for fixing. Because of unequal distribution of smartphones and use of the app across social classes, the unintended result was an inequitable provision of municipal services (Podesta, 2014).

All egalitarian views involve hard questions regarding how to address and remedy existing historical injustice. The use of algorithms in social institutions can reflect and reinforce existing inequity—for instance, through disproportionate surveillance and policing of minorities or by assessing residents of certain neighborhoods as more likely to become criminals or less worthy of access to credit. Instead of this inegalitarian reinforcement of an unjust status quo, egalitarians will seek ways to use algorithms to identify where historical inequities produce unfair outcomes and leverage the power of algorithms to correct for these results. We will return to this theme later.

Libertarianism

Libertarianism holds that the fundamental responsibility of social institutions is to protect the free exercise of basic human rights.[9] The most basic right, the right to self-ownership, undergirds other rights, such as the rights to acquire resources through labor or exchange. Libertarians argue that social institutions are unjust if they infringe on the exercise of these rights, such as if they interfere in market transactions or oth-

---

[8]   Two influential versions of this view are put forth in Dworkin, 2000, and Cohen, 1989.

[9]   For two articulations of this view, see Locke, 1689, and Nozick, 1974.

erwise try to promote a "distributive pattern" like those supported by egalitarians.[10] In this way, libertarians view equity as fundamentally a matter of respecting processes—the exercise of rights—rather than outcomes. A libertarian might view an algorithm as equitable insofar as it protects the exercise of rights, and inequitable insofar as it violates a right, such as the right to due process.

Utilitarianism

Discussions focused on equity are most commonly associated with views of ethics that seek to identify basic rules describing our duties to one another. However, other ethical theories, including those that define the morality of actions in terms of consequences, offer perspective on equity. *Utilitarianism*, a prominent strain of this latter approach, holds that the right action is the one that maximizes overall utility. Although utilitarianism is often criticized as supporting inequitable outcomes—for instance, if utility is maximized through intuitively unfair social practices, such as slavery—utilitarians may argue that their view does capture an important sense of equity. According to utilitarianism, everyone's utility counts equally when aggregated to determine which action is utility-maximizing. In this way, utilitarianism may be considered impartial, as no one person's preferences count more than any other person's, and thereby equity is ensured for all persons. With respect to algorithms, utilitarianism provides a straightforward fairness-assessment calculus, depending on whether or not the use of the algorithm maximizes utility. For a utilitarian, decisionmaking processes that use algorithms matter only as they relate to valued outcomes.

There are a multitude of additional philosophical views, but the concepts described above provide the vocabulary that informed our assessment of algorithmic equity and inspired the legal and statistical concepts described below.

Legal Concepts of Equity

Equity has a specific definition in the context of the law. It refers to particular remedies available in civil cases that are contrasted with legal remedies, or which may be available when a legal remedy is inadequate. *Legal remedies* generally involve monetary damages, while *equitable remedies* include injunctions, requiring a party to perform an act (specific performance), undoing a transaction (recission), and setting aside a judgement (vacatur). Although it is a less specific term, "fairness" may be the legal ideal most relevant to the questions raised here.

Fairness is a basic U.S. Constitutional ideal, and most Constitutional questions arise from the broad standards of fairness described in the Constitution. The key Constitutional provision invoked when considering fundamental fairness is that of due

---

[10] The critique of distributive patterns is from Nozick, 1974.

process.[11] *Procedural* and *substantive due process* are both important when considering fairness under the law. As the name suggests, procedural due process involves the requirement for notice and a hearing before the government can deprive someone of liberty or property. Substantive due process guarantees those rights that are included in the concept of "liberty;" this concept allows courts to review legislation for issues with its content, not just with application. The Fifth Amendment guarantees due process under federal law, and the 14th Amendment guarantees due process under state law.

The 14th Amendment also guarantees equal protection of the laws, which is another principle that heavily implicates fairness.[12] Due process emphasizes fairness in the relationship between an individual and the state; equal protection emphasizes fairness in the treatment of individuals who are similarly situated.

The fairness norm embodied by due process and equal protection is *nondiscrimination*. Other common concerns when assessing fairness under the law are accuracy and proportionality. Due process and accuracy can be in tension or even direct conflict; for instance, evidence may clearly indicate the guilt of a defendant, but if it was illegally gathered, due process necessitates that that evidence be ruled inadmissible.

Statistical Concepts of Equity

Recent explorations of equity in algorithms have identified a few mathematical standards of fairness that are applicable in different settings (see Table 2.1). This increased

Table 2.1
Summary of the Simpler Statistical Concepts of Equity

Statistical Concept	Formula
Fairness through unawareness (FTU)	$T = f(\{X_i\}_i), \; X_i \neq A \forall i$
Individual fairness (IF)	$T(X) \approx T(\bar{X}) \Leftrightarrow d(X, \bar{X}) \approx 0$
Demographic parity (DP)	$P(T \mid A = a_i) = P(T) \forall i$
Equal opportunity (EO)	$P(T = 1 \mid A = a_i, Y = 1) = P(T = 1 \mid A = a_j, Y = 1) \forall i \neq j$

NOTE: Some of the statistical discussion is necessarily mathematical. We use the following variables:
P(a|b): The probability of event (a), given that event (b) is the case.
$\{X_i\}_i$: A collection of (nonsensitive) input variables for a single individual.
Y: The true value of outcome (ground truth). An example would be the true underlying credit rating of an individual.
T: The decision function—a machine learning model's estimate of the unobserved Y.
A: Sensitive attributes for an individual.

---

[11] "No person shall . . . be deprived of life, liberty, or property, without due process of law" (U.S. Const., amend. V); "[N]or shall any State deprive any person of life, liberty, or property, without due process of law" (U.S. Const., amend. XIV, §1).

[12] "[N]or shall any State . . . deny to any person within its jurisdiction the equal protection of the laws" (U.S. Const., amend. XIV, §1).

applicability makes these standards more directly available to evaluate algorithms. These concepts of fairness seek to implement or approximate different legal or philosophical concepts of equity.

Fairness Through Unawareness

FTU is a mathematical interpretation of a common legal standard of procedural fairness. EO statutes aim to prevent institutional discrimination by requiring that decisionmaking be neutral with respect to specified individual sensitive attributes. These attributes often include race, gender, or other attributes that have been the subject of historical discrimination. In theory, this is simply equivalent to saying the decision function is functionally independent of sensitive attributes. We note that *functional independence*, meaning that sensitive attributes are not arguments of the decision function (i.e., the outcome is calculated without using the sensitive attributes as inputs) does not imply *statistical independence* (i.e., the outcome is uncorrelated with sensitive attributes).

FTU forces a similar form of attribute blindness on algorithms. It is an attempt to simulate a limited version of Rawls's "veil of ignorance" for algorithmic decisionmaking. FTU refers to the exclusion of sensitive attributes as inputs into a decision algorithm (Dwork et al., 2012). Consideration is still required about what actually constitutes a sensitive attribute. As a matter of practice, easily observable factors that do not reflect the choices of subjects (e.g., gender, race) typically count as sensitive attributes. This hews closer to the luck-egalitarian's perspective, but it is not a perfect alignment, as less easily observed attributes may not be included (e.g., socioeconomic status, cultural factors).

Individual Fairness

IF is a generalization of FTU. A model is individually fair if it assigns similar outcomes to individuals who are similar. The similarity measure $(d(X,\bar{X}))$ is often judged in terms of the claim *type*[13] of the individuals or claimants. In practice, judgments of similarity would exclude sensitive attributes that are superfluous to the decision outcome.[14]

Both FTU and IF emphasize a process-focused concept of fairness akin to "equal treatment." These are procedural equity norms that instantiate an egalitarian concept of equity. FTU represents the idea that individuals may not be subject to unequal treatment on the basis of attributes over which they have no control or choice. IF represents the idea that equal individuals are treated equally.

---

[13]   A person's claim type denotes all the relevant factors used to judge their desert or entitlement in a given allocation application. It *is* application-dependent.

[14]   The business necessity test of *Griggs v. Duke Power Co.* is an example of such a similarity judgment for the purpose of employment decisions (*Griggs v. Duke Power Co.*, 1971).

FTU and IF have similar disadvantages. The main one is they are not fully able to address the *proxy variable inference* concern for machine learning models. By proxy variable inference, we mean the use of available secondary unrestricted variables (e.g., home ZIP code) to get probabilistic estimates (often using machine learning models) of restricted variables (e.g. ethnicity). Recent work is beginning to show the importance of observing or recording information on sensitive attributes to improve both the equity and efficiency of algorithms (Kleinberg et al., 2018; Hardt, Price, and Srebro, 2016). Knowing the sensitive attribute status of an individual can help algorithm designers improve the fairness of their models (e.g., by using demographically specific submodels to achieve the same error rates across demographic groups).

Demographic Parity

An algorithm exhibits DP if the distribution of positive or desirable decision outcomes (e.g., getting a home loan, *not* being classified as high crime risk) mirrors the general population class distribution. DP is equivalent to having the algorithm's outcomes be statistically independent of class membership.

This is a more restrictive condition than it first appears, particularly when ground truth outcome rates are not uniform over the different classes. Class-conditional outcome uniformity tends to be highly unusual for all but the most trivial decisions. Using DP gives the class membership signal too much leverage in a decision—often to the detriment of accuracy or efficiency. But DP is often the most discussed equity standard (e.g., for employment, hiring, recruitment, and retention decisions).

A decision model that does not satisfy DP is likely to lead to representational harms, as decision outcomes that are not demographically representative can result in benefits (or burdens) distributed in a demographically unrepresentative way. This form of representational harm may not always be immediately connected with distributive concerns.

Equal Opportunity and Equalized Odds

Formally, EO is the property of having equal true positive rates across all relevant classes (Hardt, Price, and Srebro, 2016). EO is a relaxation of the more restrictive condition (equalized odds), which requires the same classification accuracy rates and misclassification rates across all classes. The statistical understanding of EO is akin to the legal concept by the same name—they both aim to guarantee access to a benefit in a way that is statistically independent of sensitive attributes (e.g., gender, race). Equalized odds guarantee that access to both benefits and harms are statistically independent of sensitive attributes.

Counterfactual Fairness

Counterfactual fairness (CF) requires the observer to hypothesize a causal model of the world (Kusner et al., 2017). This causal model may consist of both unobservable and observable variables (e.g., student grade point average, raw ability) that influence the observable outcome in focus (e.g., college admission). An algorithm is counterfactually fair if its outcome remains unchanged when sensitive attributes are changed in the causal world model. Like FTU, CF attempts to simulate a limited version of the "veil of ignorance," but it uses the hypothesized causal world model to try to account for the systemic consequences of changing the attribute class of a decision subject. CF is a causal, more-sophisticated version of EO—but crucially, the hypothesized causal world model must be valid.

For example, suppose we want to create a counterfactually fair model for college admissions. We provisionally grant that we understand the full network of causal relationships among relevant observable (e.g., gender, race, school grades, SAT scores, extracurriculars) and unobservable (e.g., ability, studiousness, resilience) factors. A university may want its admissions process to be counterfactually fair given a set of observable decision input signals by ensuring that admission probabilities remain unchanged if we plug in different values of sensitive attributes (in this case, gender and race). However, we must take into account that changes in the sensitive attributes have causal effects on the other unobserved decision-relevant factors.[15]

Asymmetry in Decisionmaking Costs

None of our statistical framings of fairness has dealt directly with issues of differences in the cost of decisionmaking. There are often asymmetric costs associated with false positive or false negative errors—for example, a false positive error by a smoke detector may lead to annoyance, but a false negative error may lead to death. The literature on Bayesian decision theory (Raiffa and Schlaifer, 1961) and cost-sensitive learning address asymmetry in costs via a risk estimate informed by an explicit cost function and some of the class-conditional probabilities introduced above. We can extend some of these statistical concepts of equity by balancing class-conditional expected costs, instead of just class-specific probabilities.

Equity in Practice: Impossibilities and Trade-Offs

The multiple perspectives on equity may be viewed as the result of different scholarly traditions trying to grasp a broad and relatively nebulous concept. It is possible to translate equity concepts among the different traditions. For example, FTU and IF can be viewed as statistical formalizations aimed at implementing legal concepts of equal treatment (or at diagnosing disparate treatment violations). They aim to quantitatively highlight when otherwise-similar people or groups receive different treatments. As

---

[15] This explicit causal calculus is a key innovation in CF, but it is also the most fraught aspect of CF. There are often unobserved or unknown confounding factors in any proposed causal account of social life. The standard approach for modeling causal webs (conditional probabilities on a directed acyclic graph) does not easily accommodate feedback loops among causal factors—and causal feedback is a standard feature of social life.

another example, researchers explored algorithmic implications of the legal concept of disparate impact, as instantiated by the U.S. Equal Employment Opportunity Commission (EEOC) "four-fifths rule" (Feldman et al., 2015; Biddle, undated):

$$\frac{P(T=1\,|\,A=0)}{(T=1\,|\,A=1)} \leq 80\%$$

where T is the prediction outcome and A is a sensitive attribute indicating protected-class membership (T = 1 is an advantageous outcome). The equation is meant to capture the disparate impact condition that members of the protected-class members (A = 1) are at least 20 percent more likely to enjoy a positive outcome (T = 1) based on the decision model producing T. These cross-disciplinary conceptual translations are rarely precise.

The plurality of perspectives on equity has implications besides imprecision in cross-domain translation. The mathematical framing of equity criteria is fruitful in forcing a more theoretical understanding of the relationships between the different equity concepts. One of the more notable sets of findings from this mathematical perspective shows that it is often *impossible* to simultaneously satisfy multiple normatively justifiable concepts of algorithmic fairness (Berk et al., 2017b). For example, a prediction model cannot be both fairly calibrated *and* have balanced error rates across the different groups.[16]

Decisionmaking models will also typically exhibit a *trade-off* between accuracy (often a measure of predictive accuracy) and fairness (Kleinberg, Mullainathan, and Raghavan, 2016). Enforcing a fairness constraint will often impose a cost on model accuracy.[17] Model designers are thus engaged in a constrained optimization exercise: Optimize the model subject to the governing equity criterion (e.g., in Berk et al., 2017a; Hardt, Price, and Srebro, 2016). Optimal models will thus operate at points along a Pareto-efficient frontier for a trade-off between accuracy and equity.

These difficulties (impossibility of simultaneous satisfaction and accuracy-fairness trade-offs) mean there are a few normative decisions that need resolution when deploying a decisionmaking artifact:

- What controlling normative concept of equity governs this decisionmaking model?

---

[16] I.e., predictive accuracy is the same across groups (Chouldechova, 2017; Kleinberg, Mullainathan, and Raghavan, 2016).

[17] This trade-off gives rise to what some researchers refer to as the *price of fairness* (Bertsimas, Farias, and Trichakis, 2011). This is the marginal reduction in model accuracy relative to a marginal increase in enforcement of a fairness constraint. Or the accuracy loss under a fair decision compared with the decision that maximizes accuracy.

- How are the equity criteria implemented mathematically?
- What is the acceptable trade-off between efficiency and equity?

These questions are not just abstract concerns. We next explore a real-world example that highlights competing concepts of fairness in a specific algorithmic manifestation and that underscores the need for a framework to address these issues.

Competing Concepts of Equity: The Case of COMPAS

The COMPAS risk assessment algorithm has been the subject of extensive debate, raising philosophical, legal, and technical questions about algorithmic equity.

COMPAS assesses the risk that a subject will commit another crime following release from custody, rating subjects on a score of one (least likely) to ten (most likely to reoffend). The risk score is determined by a set of 137 questions that relate to "criminogenic" factors, such as residence, employment stability, social isolation, and attitudes toward crime. Although the race of the subject is not explicitly assessed, gender is included, as are factors correlated with race, such as family criminal history.

In 2016, ProPublica published an analysis of COMPAS risk scores of more than 7,000 people in Broward County, Florida, in which it identified racial disparities in the algorithm's outcomes (Angwin et al., 2016). Specifically, the authors found that black defendants were twice as likely as white defendants to be falsely assessed as having a high risk of recidivism. In other words, the COMPAS outcomes for black people had almost double the false positive rate than for white people. This imbalance of group-specific error rates—a failure of the EO technical concept described above—is intuitively a sharp signal of racial inequity.[18] Consider the perspective of a black defendant facing sentencing who faces a higher probability of a harsh sentence simply because he or she is not white. From this point of view, COMPAS fails a compelling measure of equity.

In its response to ProPublica, Northpointe (now Equivant), the company that designs and sells COMPAS, raised questions about ProPublica's statistical analysis and defended the algorithm's accuracy (Dieterich, Mendoza, and Brennan, 2016). However, its key objection was that ProPublica wrongly used error rate imbalance between black and white defendants as a measure of equity.[19] Northpointe noted that because the base rate of criminality between black and white people is different—that is, black people are arrested for crimes at a greater rate than white people—an accurate risk

---

[18] Note that this does not entail that saying error rate balance is sufficient for an equitable outcome—even if equalized, this would not necessarily ensure equity.

[19] "The [ProPublica] article primarily focuses on *Model Errors* and presents these as evidence of racial bias" (Dieterich, Mendoza, and Brennan, 2016).

assessment will inevitably have unequal error rates.[20] It argued that the use of racial error rate imbalance as a critique of the algorithm is problematic, as those errors "are of no practical use to a practitioner in criminal justice agency who is assessing an offender's probability of recidivating" (Dieterich, Mendoza, and Brennan, 2016). This practical usability and predictive accuracy is the whole point of a risk assessment. Taking the perspective of a courtroom end user, Northpointe argued that COMPAS has not been shown to produce inequity.

This debate highlights two perspectives—those of the defendant and those of the court—that undergird incompatible formalizations of equity. Reconciling these competing technical notions under a more general societywide concept will not be easy. Moreover, this is just the beginning of the plurality of equity concepts at play with COMPAS.

Legal Questions About Procedural Equity

COMPAS is a proprietary tool developed by a for-profit company, and neither the defendant nor the court can examine the algorithm to understand how it weighs factors to produce a risk score. In addition, COMPAS takes gender explicitly into account as part of its risk assessment—a factor that in other contexts is considered a protected category that cannot be the basis for disparate treatment.[21]

In the case of *State of Wisconsin v. Eric Loomis*, the Supreme Court of Wisconsin was asked whether the use of the COMPAS algorithm by a sentencing court violated the due process clause of the 14th Amendment of the Constitution. In its decision, the court reasoned that the use of COMPAS in this specific case did not violate due process because the defendant's sentence was based on other factors in addition to the COMPAS score.[22] Furthermore, they stated that COMPAS provides sufficient transparency, as defendants have access to the questions that the algorithm considers in its assessment. With respect to the use of gender as a risk factor, the court decided that it was entirely appropriate, reasoning that "if the inclusion of gender promotes accuracy, it serves the interests of institutions and defendants, rather than a discriminatory purpose."[23]

---

[20]   This is proven in Chouldechova, 2017, which shows that if an algorithm like COMPAS satisfies predictive parity and the base rate is different for different groups, then the algorithm cannot achieve equal false positive and false negative rates across groups.

[21]   For instance, the Civil Rights Act identifies gender as a protected category (along with race, religion, and so forth).

[22]   The due process clause is usually interpreted to mean that a sentencing court cannot use factors that are "constitutionally impermissible or totally irrelevant to the sentencing process," such as race or religion (*Zant v. Stephens*, 1983). The State of Wisconsin itself prohibits sentencing "because of" gender, but the court noted that the Loomis sentencing decision was not "because of" gender.

[23]   *State v. Loomis*, 2016 (citing Hamilton, 2015). However, as the court stated, "Notably . . . Loomis does not bring an equal protection challenge in this case," suggesting that it might have been more inclined to find a viola-

The court relied on New York state's analysis of the COMPAS tool to conclude that it was sufficiently accurate, although it recognized that it was not in a position to evaluate the reliability of the data.[24] It also acknowledged that COMPAS had not yet been validated on a Wisconsin population. Although it is not part of the holding, the court addressed the fact that New York and other states had assessed COMPAS's predictive accuracy for recidivism, while Wisconsin was using it as a factor in determining sentence length. As discussed below, and as acknowledged by the Wisconsin court, sentencing decisions are more complex and serve additional goals as compared with pretrial detention or probation decisions. The court affirmed that

> risk scores may not be used: (1) to determine whether an offender is incarcerated; or (2) to determine the severity of the sentence. Additionally, risk scores may not be used as the determinative factor in deciding whether an offender can be supervised safely and effectively in the community (*State v. Loomis*, 2016).

The Loomis case ends there, but the broader procedural equity questions remain and will likely be the focus of sustained legal debate. Is it fair to impacted persons that public institutions use proprietary and opaque tools to inform consequential decisions? Consider again the perspective of defendants unable to mitigate specific factors associated with their score because they do not and cannot understand how the algorithm weighs them.

In addition, the use of sensitive categories in serious decisions creates procedural issues. The existence of systemic historical and present-day racial injustice underscores an intuition among egalitarians and others that race should not be used to assess recidivism risk, even if that promotes accuracy. Data analytics facilitates the discovery and close association of race and proxy variables, which makes it difficult to simply blacklist certain protected variables. The explicit or implicit use of race, gender, or other variables might improve algorithmic accuracy in the sense of matching base rate criminality, but that raises questions about the importance of protecting certain sensitive attributes and poses a risk of disparate mistreatment. In the case of COMPAS, the goal of using an accurate algorithm that reflects preexisting conditions seems to be at odds with goals associated with equity.

---

tion under that argument regarding the use of gender in the COMPAS metric.

[24] The New York analysis used signal detection analysis to plot a receiver operating characteristic curve, and used the area under the curve as a measure of accuracy. The area under the curve's value can range from 0.50 to 1.00; values near 0.50 have little to no predictive accuracy, the 0.60s have low to moderate predictive accuracy, the 0.70s have satisfactory predictive accuracy, and 0.80 and above is evidence of strong predictive accuracy. The area under the curve for the COMPAS measure was 0.71, so COMPAS's accuracy was rated as satisfactory. See Lansing, 2012.

Philosophical Considerations

More philosophically, there is a question of whether courts that use COMPAS should simply accept base rate differences of criminality due to race. According to the algorithm developers, COMPAS is viewed by courts as successful when it accurately reflects these base rates. However, as Rawls and other egalitarian philosophers have argued, race is morally arbitrary and should not factor into the probability that one is in jail or free. By accurately reflecting base rate criminality and thereby treating black people as higher risk than white people, COMPAS perpetuates a disproportionate impact along racial lines. Indeed, a high COMPAS score even creates feedback that increases racial differences in base rate criminality. If existing base rates are unjust (because of historical factors and structural racism), it can be argued that accurate algorithms, such as COMPAS, are complicit in and contribute to this societywide injustice.[25] This is an example of how reliance on automated decisionmaking models can entrench preexisting systemic inequities.

Equity is not the only value that matters in criminal justice contexts, and technical research has shown that maximizing equitable outcomes with COMPAS poses costs to public safety.[26] In these cases, social institutions must consider how to reconcile different and potentially opposing societywide goals.

COMPAS Implementation Issues

Finally, equity and other normative issues also arise with how COMPAS is used in practice. The Loomis decision was based in part on the fact that COMPAS was not used to determine sentences, but it is not clear that this is the case everywhere.[27] Indeed, ProPublica found a case in which a judge overturned a plea deal and imposed harsher sentences because of a high COMPAS score.[28] The risks of automation bias

---

[25] The argument that base rate differences in criminality should not be justly accepted by social institutions is controversial. Libertarian philosophers, for instance, might argue that social institutions must protect individual rights in a way that would preclude them from any infringements that would modify base rates.

[26] Optimizing for fairness in COMPAS risk assessment (1) requires detaining more low-risk defendants and (2) reduces public safety by increasing the risk of violent crime: "There are tangible costs to satisfying popular notions of algorithmic fairness" (Corbett-Davies et al., 2017).

[27] Note that COMPAS is intended "to be used to identify offenders who could benefit from interventions and to target risk factors that should be addressed during supervision." It is "[n]ot intended to determine the severity of the sentence or whether an offender is incarcerated" (*State v. Loomis*, 2016).

[28] From Angwin et al., 2016:

> The first time Paul Zilly heard of his score — and realized how much was riding on it — was during his sentencing hearing on February 15, 2013, in court in Barron County, Wisconsin. Zilly had been convicted of stealing a push lawnmower and some tools. The prosecutor recommended a year in county jail and follow-up supervision that could help Zilly with "staying on the right path." His lawyer agreed to a plea deal. But Judge James Babler had seen Zilly's scores. Northpointe's software had rated Zilly as a high risk for future violent crime and a medium risk for general recidivism. "When I look at the risk assessment," Babler said in court, "it is about

are relevant here, especially as the COMPAS creators claim that COMPAS provides evidence-based outcomes that ameliorate human bias.

Even if not determinative, different courts give COMPAS assessments different weights. Any assessment of COMPAS's equity would have to take into account variance across practices and the discretion that judges have in using COMPAS information.

In its decision on Loomis, the Wisconsin Supreme Court identified ways that COMPAS should be constrained in practice, noting that there needs to be a "written advisement listing [its] limitation" and that "risk assessment tools must be constantly monitored and re-normed for accuracy due to changing populations and subpopulations." There are almost certainly other implementation practices that need to be considered for fair outcomes.

Metaethical Aspects of Algorithmic Equity

Given the varied concepts of equity, it is likely impossible to make an objective argument for one prescriptive concept of equity from first principles, and we will not be arguing in favor of any specific approach in general or specific different cases. We can highlight key aspects of such a metaethical approach.

Value Pluralism

Our primary goal is to point out the range of competing reasonable fairness values (*value pluralism*; Berlin, 2000). As much as possible, we evaluate equity claims from within the norms of existing social institutions rather than from an abstract prescriptive philosophical perspective. Norms within institutions are shaped by stakeholders' moral intuitions, culture, and explicit (or implicit) regulations. These institutional norms are often tuned (sometimes very imperfectly) to negotiate among the different individual values in order to gain user buy-in or legitimacy.

Voice and Avenues for Dissent

Value pluralism is not the end point of our investigation. There is also the *metaethical* question of what mechanisms can be designed to better tune institutions so that they align better with stated institutional values or norms. A crucial step here is the ability to listen to and understand stakeholders' concerns.

Stakeholders' equity concerns are a necessarily *distributed* form of knowledge; a single controller is unlikely to have all such knowledge a priori. The decentralized nature of equity concerns and the diversity of equity norms at play in an institution highlight the importance of having effective channels for dissent. Stakeholders need

---

as bad as it could be." Then Babler overturned the plea deal that had been agreed on by the prosecution and defense and imposed two years in state prison and three years of supervision.

to be able to voice equity concerns from their independent perspectives. Any decision-making process that does not enable meaningful effective dissent allows for potential unaddressed concerns.

Some institutions have explicit mechanisms to facilitate the expression of views and that allow affected parties to contest decisions. These participatory mechanisms are crucial to ensure that the full range of equity perspectives is addressed.

Procedures for Accountable Redress

Further elaboration would include other institutional mechanisms that allow alignment of the interests of individual participants. Minimal requirements for effective institutional adaptation might include such factors as transparency in guiding norms, avenues for voicing dissent without excessive friction, and stable adaptive procedures for responding effectively to equity challenges. We examine these considerations in more detail through the case studies in the following chapters.

Understanding Necessary Trade-Offs

As a further scoping framework, it is useful to point out that the tensions highlighted among reasonable governing equity values (e.g., in the COMPAS discussion) are not without precedent. These tensions mirror similar tensions among equity values in collective choice systems formalized in Kenneth Arrow's Impossibility Theorem and its corollaries many decades ago (Arrow, 2012; Sen, 2018).[29] Those impossibility results now help inform principled mechanism design for collective choice (e.g., electoral systems and auctions) by bounding what is possible and what trade-offs are necessary. The algorithmic equity impossibility results discussed earlier can begin to serve a similar purpose for algorithmic decisionmaking.

---

[29]   Specifically, for collective choice via voting, a notional *fair* voting mechanism would be nondictatorial, able to adjudicate among *any* set of individual preferences, pareto-optimal, and indifferent to preferences on irrelevant alternatives.

CHAPTER THREE

Domain Exploration: Algorithms in Auto Insurance

Private insurance markets serve an important social function by helping individuals hedge against catastrophic personal risk.[1] The classical justification in economic theory for the existence of insurance markets is *risk aversion*—the desire to reduce financial exposure to uncertain adverse events. Risk aversion is a sufficient condition for a consumer to purchase actuarially fair insurance against any risk, if such insurance is available.[2] (Perfectly actuarially fair insurance is essentially never available for purchase because of administrative expenses and imperfectly competitive insurance markets, among other real-world complications.) The robustness of insurance markets despite the unavailability of actuarially fair insurance suggests that consumer demand for risk protection is extremely widespread.

Real-world insurance markets are also subject to price distortions caused by asymmetric information. One widely known form of market failure caused by asymmetric information is *adverse selection*. Adverse selection is a market failure that occurs when consumers have superior information about their probability or expected severity of losses in comparison with the insurer. In recent decades, economists have made major advances in the theoretical and empirical analysis of adverse selection. A major theme of this literature is that the presence, magnitude, and welfare implications of adverse selection are very sensitive to the information structure and regulatory environment of the particular market in question. The risks being insured and the nature of consumer demand for insurance coverage also play a role. The impact of adverse selection on social welfare must be evaluated empirically on a market-by-market basis and thus is a fundamentally empirical question (Cohen and Siegelman, 2010).

---

[1] The Organization for Economic Cooperation and Development reports that spending on private insurance by U.S. households and businesses (measured as direct gross premiums) was 11.3 percent of gross domestic product in 2016 (Organization for Economic Cooperation and Development, 2018).

[2] In fact, risk aversion is logically equivalent to the property of having nonzero demand for actuarially fair insurance under all circumstances. However, we would call this a sufficient condition and not a necessary condition because one can imagine behavioral-economic justifications for insurance purchase even by non–risk-averse, even risk-loving, agents. A sufficient degree of pessimism (in terms of systematically overestimating the risk of the insured loss occurring so that insurance purchase is misperceived as having an expected value that exceeds the premium), for example, would lead a non–risk-averse agent to purchase insurance.

Insurance pricing may *seem* to present a trade-off between market efficiency and fairness. In order to remain solvent and fulfill the function of protecting consumers from financial risk, insurers must collect enough premiums to cover the cost of claims. When consumers have information about their expected losses, more-detailed risk classification may be necessary to prevent welfare losses due to adverse selection. *Actuarially fair* insurance pricing (in the sense of pricing that is commensurate to individually calibrated risk) is often contrasted with the need for insurance pricing that is "fair" or equitable (in the demographic parity sense). But the American Academy of Actuaries argues that the risk of consumers "adversely selecting" in a competitive *voluntary* insurance market makes the goals of market efficiency and fairness more synergistic (American Academy of Actuaries, Risk Classification Work Group, 2011).

This points to the challenge of formalizing fairness in the context of insurance. We can ground a rough concept of fairness in insurance pricing in the requirement that differences in insurance prices reflect only differences in risk evaluation. This means that although insurance prices are supposed to be primarily discriminatory relative to risk-relevant signals, they should be functionally independent of risk-irrelevant signals, particularly when regulatory fiat designates these signals as "sensitive."[3] This concept of fairness mirrors the American Academy of Actuaries' definition of fairness (termed "individual equity") in risk classification, as discussed in their monograph on risk classification and statement of principles (American Academy of Actuaries, Committee on Risk Classification, undated). There are a few structural mechanisms that can promote fairness-like requirements: the legal or regulatory regime, a competitive insurance market, and public perception.

Insurers and regulators aim to have an insurance market that is efficient, solvent, and equitable (in the default sense of individual equity or in a broader sense of social adequacy or justice). The advent of complex algorithmic decision aids complicates matters. Such algorithmic aids include AI and machine learning models that may be useful for insurance underwriting, risk adjustment, or rate-setting. These tools promise better efficiency, accuracy, and consistency in risk calibration. But the opacity of many such algorithmic decision aids (i.e., the difficulty of identifying reasons or causes for their automated decisions) can be problematic in insurance pricing. A large part of the tensions exists because these complex models have a growing capacity to circumvent social adequacy rules about the use of sensitive attributes.

---

[3]   The concept of risk relevance is also somewhat shaky. Signals could be informative with respect to risk in a causal or purely associational/correlational fashion. The difference in these modes of relevance takes on increased salience, as machine learning models excel at association and struggle with causal relationships.

The Auto Insurance Decision Pipeline

In this section, we explore the roles of algorithms in insurance markets and some of the regulatory mechanisms that exist to oversee the use of algorithms. We will be limiting our attention to auto insurance.

The auto insurance market in the United States is subject to state-level regulation. State insurance commissioners coordinate on best practices and standards for insurance regulation via membership in the national regulatory standards body, the National Association of Insurance Commissioners. However, significant diversity exists between state regulatory schemes. Insurance commissioners' offices vet disclosures by insurers operating in their state. Some states require insurers to obtain *prior approval* for their rate-setting formulae. Others take a more laissez-faire approach to regulation, adopting a "file-and-use" approach (without requiring prior approval). There are few variations between these two approaches.

Besides rate-filing procedures, states have different restrictions on what are allowable variables to use in rate-setting for auto insurance. States have varying degrees of restrictions on rate discrimination on the basis of such attributes as race, gender, religion, and national origin (see Figure 3.1; Avraham, Logue, and Schwarcz, 2014a, 2014b).

Summary of Decision Stages

What follows is an overview of some steps in the auto insurance market process (see Figure 3.2). Many of the steps involve the use of statistical models and algorithms, some of which are proprietary or only disclosed to state regulators.

Marketing and advertising. Insurers start with decisions on how to target viable consumers with advertising. There are algorithms in use in this phase. But the use of algorithms in the advertising ecosystem is a deep and complex line of inquiry that extends outside the scope of this discussion (and outside the scope of just insurance).

Underwriting. There is also a process of identifying variables and characteristics that are relevant to or predictive of expected cost (Actuarial Standards Board, 2011). The goal is to enable *risk classification*: the principled assignment of individual risk to classes based on specific and definite attributes (American Academy of Actuaries, Risk Classification Work Group, 2011). This requires consultation with actuaries and, sometimes, domain experts (especially for more-exotic insurance products). Underwriting models are often proprietary or classified as trade secrets. Good underwriting models make an insurer competitive relative to its peers. A key component of the underwriting process is the decision whether or not to issue insurance to a consumer at all (in any possible risk class).

Rate-setting is the process of setting prices for actual insurance contracts for individuals or groups of individuals. Different insurers will use different formulas to set these rates. And the efficiency of insurance markets depends on insurers' ability to

Figure 3.1
State Auto Insurance Regulatory Regimes

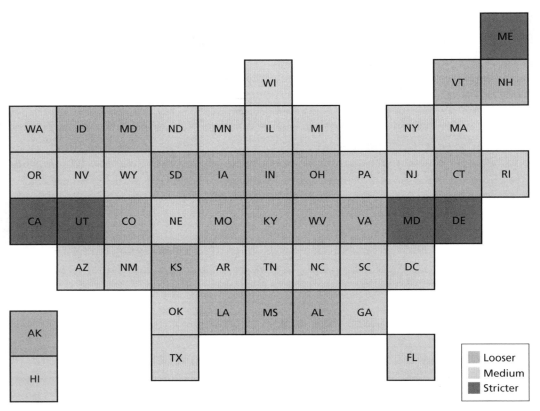

SOURCE: RAND research based on data from Avraham, Logue, and Schwarcz, 2014a.
NOTE: Each regime represents a cluster of states based on the similarity in how they regulate the use of sensitive attributes (e.g., age, gender, race, religion, sexual orientation). Red states tend to have more-prescriptive regulations, while green states have looser regulations (yellow states fall in the middle).

accurately price risk classes and set commensurate premiums in a way that is competitive. States often require insurers to disclose their rate-setting formulae and the variables that go into them; the formulae can be rather complex.

Price optimization is an elaboration on the rate-setting procedure in which an insurer modifies or assigns insurance rates based on factors that have no causal or correlative relevance to the customer's insurance risk (National Association of Insurance Commissioners, 2015). Insurers sometimes use this procedure to benefit from differences in consumer price sensitivities (or their "price elasticity of demand"). Some states have taken positions against this practice, while others have chosen to regulate overall market behavior.

Price and risk adjustment. A basic assumption in risk classification is that risk classes are a stable estimate of consumers' probabilistic risk. But, in practice, risk classes

Figure 3.2
Notional Rendition of the Auto Insurance Decision Pipeline

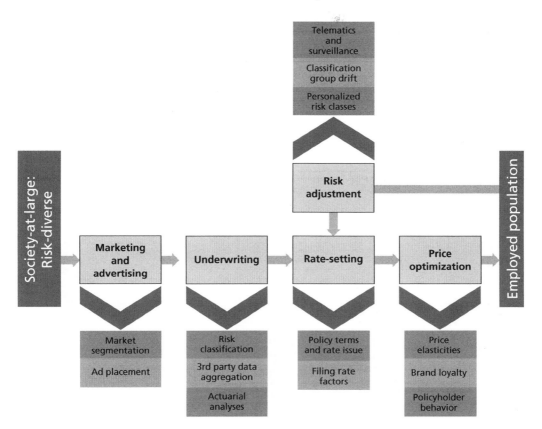

are dynamic and can evolve over time to become poorly predictive to actual observed risk groups. This sort of classification change often occurs simply over time because of the aging of risk groups cohorts. However, the increasing use of new information sources or telematic devices (e.g., driving monitoring devices, health monitoring) can reveal finer-grained signals that can allow estimates on previously unobservable latent risk factors.

Algorithmic or automated decisionmaking aids can feature in many stages of this decision pipeline. Insurers already use complex formulae to set rates based on allowable rate factors and, in some cases, secondary factors. Automated underwriting already exists in some other types of insurance schemes. For example, reporting on automated underwriting tools for risk classification in mortgage lending revealed that these automated tools actually improved outcomes for underserved demographics (Gates, Perry, and Zorn, 2002).

Relevant Concepts of Equity in Auto Insurance

The concept of equity in the auto insurance domain is somewhat different from due process or equal treatment concepts of fairness that guide such domains as criminal justice. Fair insurance pricing in a voluntary market (or in a compulsory market with *elements of choice*) will be necessarily discriminatory with respect to risk[4] if the insurance market is going to be efficient or self-sustaining; individuals with the same, or approximately the same, level of risk should get the same risk classification and the same rate:

$$P(T\,|\,\dot{R}(X_a)=r)=P(T\,|\,R(X_b)=r),$$

in which R(.) represents a function of characteristics that predict a consumer's expected losses.[5] This is a form of IF in which individuals are compared on the basis of a similarity score that matches people in the same risk class.

This concept of equity is similar to the idea of a subsidy-free cost-sharing solution in a cost-sharing game (Young, 1995, p. 88; Moulin, 2004, p. 139). In a cost-sharing game, agents pool resources (e.g., insurance premiums) to defray the cost of a joint venture (e.g., the cost of probable adverse events) that benefits each agent to different degrees (e.g., each agent's risk propensities). A solution to a cost-sharing game is subsidy-free if each agent's contribution is proportional to the cost he or she imposes on the joint venture—i.e., agents contribute premiums that are proportional to how much risk they impose relative to the rest of the group. The difference here is the game is coordinated by the insurer, who aims to extract some profit on the margins.

The American Academy of Actuaries argues that this risk-discriminative concept of fairness must be the default controlling concept for voluntary insurance schemes if insurance companies are to provide a sufficient product and keep sufficient resources to stay solvent.[6] We may qualify the claim of individual equity as the "default con-

---

[4]   There are alternate concepts of what norms should govern an insurance scheme. Involuntary insurance schemes, for example, prioritize the full participation of the relevant demographic over risk fairness. Such involuntary schemes typically feature government subsidies to keep the market solvent (e.g., subsidized auto insurance for low-income participants who cannot afford their risk-fair premiums).

[5]   An interesting feature of the insurance rate-setting problem from a modeling point of view is that the model outcome or decision variable (Y) can be cast as either a binary or a continuous variable. Of course, underwriting and rate-setting are actually joint decisions available to the insurer in response to any change in the business environment. Underwriting regulations can frequently be offset (or undone entirely) through rate-setting, and vice versa. Auto insurance has separate, complex laws and regulations regarding underwriting and rate-setting, and a detailed or empirical analysis of AI in auto insurance is beyond the scope of this report.

[6]   The American Academy of Actuaries highlights three criteria necessary for the success of a subsidy-free insurance scheme. The second of the criteria is that coverage terms are acceptable to eligible participants. The writers elaborate on this criterion:

trolling concept" by highlighting the fact that insurance schemes may be designed to emphasize other social adequacy criteria besides individual equity (e.g., affordability). These adaptations may necessitate the use of internal or external subsidies to sustain the insurance market over time.

The primary argument for relevance of individual equity is the problem of adverse selection. The information asymmetry that makes adverse selection possible may occur because of regulatory rate-setting restrictions that blacklist variables that are predictive[7] of risk. The information asymmetry may also simply be due to privately withheld information (e.g., undisclosed preexisting conditions). Adverse selection behaviors reduce the efficiency of insurance schemes by causing mispriced risks.

Voluntary insurance schemes that violate individual equity will experience adverse selection in the form of overpriced (i.e., less risky) clients choosing to opt out while underpriced (i.e., more risky) clients opt in. The average observed covered risk of the insurance pool will then rise, leading in turn to rising premiums to cover payouts. This is a price spiral that can become unsustainable (without external subsidies).

Social adequacy criteria in insurance schemes may be construed to include every other mandated goal besides individual equity, solvency, and profitability. Social adequacy concerns include such normative requirements as affordability, demographic anti-discrimination (e.g., on gender, race, or age), mandatory coverage, or a requirement to ignore preexisting risk-relevant factors. Enforcing these will result in equity norms that look more like EO or like equalized odds concepts of fairness.

Social adequacy requirements can reduce the market efficiency of insurance schemes if the restricted factors are predictive of expected insurance cost. The impact on market efficiency may necessitate the use of subsidies or insurance coverage mandates to keep the market functional. In general, the regulators' task is to try to balance efficiency (preventing adverse selection) and fairness (preventing illicit discrimination).

While participants all prefer a lower price, prices that are reasonably related to the perceived cost of coverage are more likely to be understood and thus to achieve broad acceptance than would prices that are not related to the perceived cost of coverage. To the extent prices for coverage within a [insurance scheme] are reasonably proportional to the corresponding expected costs of coverage, the system is said to achieve individual equity (2011, p. 3–4).

And again:

[...] potential participants are unlikely to be attracted to a security system in which price for covering [apparently] identical risks differ significantly (2011, p. 26).

Actuarial Standards Board, 2011, Section 3.2 also contains an endorsement of individually equitable risk classification as recommended practice for actuaries in the United States.

[7] "Predictive" here can refer to either the presence of a causal relationship or just a merely associative or correlational relationship. Actuarial standards of practice do not require establishing causal relationships between risk characteristics and expected cost of the individual to the insurer.

Equity Challenges

Redlining

The most common challenge is the question of *redlining*, a state of affairs in which members of geographic communities of lower socioeconomic status are charged higher insurance premiums relative to their actual insurance risk (Squires, 1998). Redlining, where it exists, violates both the individual equity requirement and the affordability social adequacy mandate. The consumers affected are precisely the ones who can ill afford the premium hike. It also raises the risk of noncompliance with mandatory insurance laws. This can lead to further expensive interactions with law enforcement in the form of fines.

The redlining equity challenge is crucially concerned with the mismatch between price and risk. The data for one factor—price—are easily observable. But the data for the other factor—observed risk—are often harder to find (often because of trade secret concerns). Many discussions observe higher premiums in subregions with lower socioeconomic status (which often closely track with minorities and immigrant communities). It is plausible that higher premiums are justified in these subregions because observed risks are higher there; this is the common response from auto insurers (Angwin et al., 2017).

However, one simulation study in the Los Angeles region found that covered insurance risks are indeed higher for people living in minority or low–socioeconomic status neighborhoods—*but* the difference in insurance premiums exceeds what is justified by the difference in risk (Ong and Stoll, 2007). A more recent study analyzed data on premium quotes *and* incurred insurance losses for states that kept ZIP code–level records of insurance payouts (Angwin et al., 2017).[8] The researchers' analyses supported the existence of redlining in California, Illinois, Missouri, and Texas, as well as in the District of Columbia. There was a stable pattern of premiums in minority-majority ZIP codes exceeding non-minority ZIP premiums, even when both groups had the same risk levels.

Sensitive Attribute Designation

Another common equity challenge in insurance is deciding which normative factors must be excluded from or included in considerations of insurance risk. There is significant state diversity on this question. State regulations run the gamut of permitting or outright banning the use of such attributes as gender, religion, sexual orientation, and age; many explicitly prohibit the use of racial categories (Avraham, Logue, and Schwarcz, 2014a).

And yet redlining along what are effectively racial categories still occurs (Young, 1995, p. 88; Moulin, 2004, p. 139). This is likely because race attributes are easily

---

8   States and districts include California, Illinois, Missouri, Texas, and Washington, D.C.

inferred from legal and sometimes innocuous secondary attributes, given enough data and training. Geographic attributes have particularly strong inferential power for identifying subjects and their characteristics (Sweeney, 2000; Golle, 2006), especially when there is significant segregation in a region (Fiscella and Fremont, 2006). New secondary data sources, such as social media data, telematics, and offerings from data brokers, may be available now or in the future to further inform underwriting or even rate-setting decisions. These extra sources of data may further telegraph prohibited attributes probabilistically. This can lead to situations in which the letter of the law is respected while the intent (i.e., nondiscrimination on the basis of supposedly sensitive attributes) is violated. Observed redlining outcomes among compliant insurers is just one such example.

Effects of Mandatory Insurance

Many states require drivers to have auto insurance. The combination of a private-sector insurance market and a universal coverage mandate can pose a dilemma for drivers who are high-risk and poor: Drive illegally or pay unaffordable premiums. This dilemma is especially difficult to resolve in states that do not offer affordable public alternatives. This scenario represents a type of undue or excess burden because of an imposed adequacy criterion (mandatory insurance). There is a discussion to be had on how to justly bear the foreseeable burdens of social adequacy criteria.

Closing Thoughts

Auto insurance is a peculiar domain for explorations of equity. There is an inherent coupling between the efficiency and equity goals of a voluntary insurance scheme. In a perfectly transparent, competitive insurance market, there would be no incentive for any form of discrimination, except on risk-relevant characteristics. Two considerations seem to complicate matters:

- **Low transparency.** Some of the information needed to judge the actuarial fairness of insurers' algorithms and models are either only partially disclosed or complete trade secrets. This includes underwriting and risk-estimation models. In some cases in which researchers inferred algorithms' structure from the available evidence (e.g., ProPublica's analysis of Illinois auto insurers), the relationship between premiums and risks was rather tenuous.
- **Regulatory blacklisting of attributes.** Regulators sometimes impose social adequacy mandates requiring that insurers do not discriminate on some attribute. Occasionally said attribute is actually informative of risk (e.g., the driver's gender). Such regulatory blacklisting would make insurers competing in the same market operate on a lower efficiency curve—unless an insurer identifies a sec-

ondary, unregulated proxy variable. Algorithmic tools are increasingly capable at extracting such proxies. Worse, the formal excision of sensitive attributes from insurer data makes it hard to examine insurance algorithms for inequitable outcomes.

CHAPTER FOUR

Domain Exploration: Algorithms in Employee Recruitment

Organizations seek to hire the most-qualified, capable talent while reducing risks and costs associated with the hiring search. Historically, humans have made all hiring decisions, including such associated tasks as writing a job description, posting availability, screening resumes and candidates, coordinating interviews, negotiating salaries and other benefits, and final onboarding. More decisions are made after hiring has occurred, such as promotions and layoffs. At each phase of this hiring pipeline, there are risks of inequity based on race, gender, or other qualities, both through intended human decisions and through seemingly neutral processes.

Today, nearly every step in the recruitment process can be automated through algorithms. These algorithms have the potential to combat many human-caused biases. Unfortunately, if insufficient consideration is given to how they are developed and implemented, they can reinforce existing inequities and even create new ones.

In one noteworthy example, in 2014 and 2015, Amazon designed and used an algorithm to help select candidate resumes. However, after an assessment, Amazon determined that the algorithm was biased against women; the training data used to teach the algorithm how to select a good candidate predominantly involved resumes from men. As a result, the algorithm learned to disfavor women (for instance, by disfavoring candidates who attended all-women's schools). This bias reinforced historical disparities, but it was the a result of the new algorithms, suggesting the need for new tools to address these issues. Amazon has abandoned that particular system, but other algorithmic recruitment systems risk having the same or similar problems (Dastin, 2018).

This chapter begins with a brief overview of equity issues in employment and the legal structures that have been put in place to prevent employment discrimination. After an explanation of the potential benefits of employment algorithms, the chapter will focus on the role of algorithms associated with one stage of the employment pipeline: candidate recruitment. The chapter will conclude with some research recommendations and suggestions on how to improve the likelihood of equitable outcomes. Rather than a technical deep dive, this chapter will provide a broader outlook on algorithmic recruiting to indicate the range of issues at play and to illustrate the need for and challenges associated with future research.

Relevant Concepts of Equity in Employment

Employment is at the core of many essential elements of human well-being, including income; health and retirement benefits; social status; and, for many, a sense of dignity and self-worth. Philosophers have long theorized about the importance and value of human labor; egalitarians especially have emphasized the principle of fair equality of opportunity, in which all people have the opportunity to develop the skills valued by employers.[1]

A wide variety of features that do not influence job performance have been demonstrated to have an impact on hiring in the United States. Some examples of characteristics that can be favored or disfavored include gender, race, age, religion, sexual orientation, immigration status, and marital status. Increased awareness of these instances of discrimination have shaped legislation and governance structures meant to curb such incidents and provide recourse. The overarching goal of these legal protections is to ensure that features specifically related to work function determine who gains employment, rather than arbitrary or nonrelevant factors. We do not discuss the complex history of antidiscrimination employment law here, but we do briefly describe some major developments relevant to algorithmic recruitment practices.

Title VII of the Civil Rights Act of 1964 prohibits discrimination against employees on the basis of *protected classes*, which now include gender, race, age, disability, color, creed, national origin, religion, and genetic information (EEOC, undated). The law prohibits intentional or overt discrimination on the basis of membership of the protected classes—a practice sometimes known as *disparate treatment*. It also protects against *disparate impact*, in which a seemingly neutral practice negatively impacts some people in a protected class more than others.[2]

Demonstrating disparate treatment and disparate impact is difficult. In the case of disparate treatment, the burden of proof falls on the employee to show discrimination through a *prima facie* case (such as through the circumstantial evidence of hearing denigrating comments from an employer). Disparate impact is also hard to demonstrate because it burdens the plaintiff to show that there is an alternative employment practice that the employer refuses to adopt that would not produce the same disparate outcome. The use of algorithms in recruitment further complicates the demonstration of disparate treatment and disparate impact—an issue we will return to later.

Following the Civil Rights Act, several important cases contributed to legal approaches to protecting equity in employment. In 1971's *Griggs v. Duke Power Co.*, the Supreme Court considered Duke Power Company's hiring requirement that indi-

---

[1]   Philosophers as varied in outlook as John Locke and Karl Marx have emphasized the importance of labor. We will not be considering broader theoretical questions about the institutional value of labor here. We instead focus on the legally codified norms discussed below.

[2]   The EEOC offers 80 percent as a practical rule for determining whether a practice has resulted in disparate impact (Biddle, undated).

viduals in upper-level positions in the company hold a high school diploma—a creden-
tial most potential black applicants did not possess. The court determined that achieve-
ment of a high school diploma was not necessary to perform the job duties in those
positions, and thus that the diploma requirement was not "reasonably related" to job
performance. Even though the policy did not explicitly reference any protected classes
and was in this way racially neutral or "colorblind," the court ruled that the disparate
impact of the policy was discriminatory. The case is often interpreted as showing that
policies that are neutral in intent cannot be maintained if they operate to "freeze" the
status quo of prior discriminatory employment practice (*Griggs v. Duke Power Co.*,
1971).

The 2009 U.S. Supreme Court case *Ricci v. DeStefano* underscores the possibility
of prima facie tension between disparate treatment and disparate impact. In this case,
firefighters (most of whom were white) at the New Haven Fire Department argued that
they were disparately treated by the city when it invalidated the results of a promotion
test. The city claimed it dismissed the test results in order to guard against charges that
the test would have had a disparate impact against black firefighters, none of whom
had scored sufficiently high enough to be considered for promotion. The city sought
to avoid disparate impact liability by invalidating the results, but thereby engaged in
disparate treatment against the firefighters who passed the test. The court held that an
employer must have a strong basis of evidence that it will be liable for disparate impact
claims in order to engage in intentional discrimination for the purpose of promoting
equitable racial outcome. The court then ruled that the city did not have sufficient evidence of that risk (*Ricci v. Destefano*, 2009).

These cases demonstrate the intricacies of determining whether employment
decisions are discriminatory, as well as of finding the type and amount of evidence
needed to demonstrate discrimination. They also demonstrate the competing concepts
of equity in employment, even within the legal concepts codified in the Civil Rights
Act and developed through case law.

Statisticians have also sought to formalize concepts of equity in employment.
Researchers have offered technical approaches to promote nondiscrimination, such
as by developing procedures to repair training data to encourage algorithms to produce a more equitable result (Ajunwa et al., 2016). Others have sought to formalize
concepts of disparate impact, such as the EEOC's 80-percent rule, to provide more-
precise detection of when disparate impact occurs and to alter data sets in such a way
to minimize it (Feldman et al., 2015). Much of the technical analysis, however, notes
that interventions in the data that seek to promote more-equitable outcomes could also
degrade the accuracy of the algorithm, thus underscoring the assumption that there are
trade-offs between accuracy and equity.

Benefits of Recruitment Algorithms

Employment algorithm developers claim to offer a variety of benefits for employers—improving accuracy and efficiency of the search, while also guarding against legal risks and promoting a more diverse workforce.

Human resources tools that evaluate potential employees are part of a $100 billion market (Alsever, 2017). Algorithms are viewed as a cheaper, faster, more-effective way to execute tasks traditionally performed by humans. Multiple startups have begun to develop new algorithmic capabilities to reduce effort, increase capabilities, and create new services. Hundreds of startups are entering the market, with more likely to emerge in the coming years.

The firms that create recruitment algorithms—and the companies that use the algorithms—often report that one of the benefits of algorithms is that they are "bias-free." By using algorithms to sift through the multitude of information about candidates, and by programming the algorithms to "ignore" protected class information, such as gender and race, companies are able to claim that they did not consider those characteristics in their hiring decisions and are thereby in compliance with anti-discrimination rules. In this way, the use of algorithms is thought to provide a hedge against legal risks associated with human searches for job candidates.

Firms also claim that algorithm use can promote diversity in the workforce. Unilever began using online targeted advertising to broaden the base of schools for potential recruits; it claimed to have tripled the number of schools it recruited from through this targeting method (Feloni, 2017). Entelo, a talent sourcing firm, stated that it had increased female hires from 40 percent to 47 percent and increased the number of minority technical hires from 1.5 percent to 11 percent at a company called Opower (Entelo, undated). Some companies even specialize in text-generating machine learning algorithms that write job descriptions intended to improve gender diversity (Textio, undated; Talvista, undated).

Companies also enjoy the economic benefits of using these services. There are claims that algorithmic recruitment processes are faster, more accurate, and result in fewer terminations, reducing the time and money spent on hiring. For example, Indigo, Canada's largest bookstore chain, stated that since utilizing the talent recruitment firm Ideal, it had experienced a 71-percent reduction in costs per hire and a "tripling of qualified candidates" (Ideal, undated).

Employment Algorithm Decision Pipeline

This section attempts to identify current practices that may develop into trends relevant to combating inequitable recruitment practices. Figure 4.1 presents a pipeline indicating the decision points across the employment process. The pipeline suggests

Figure 4.1
Notional Rendition of Decision Pipeline for Employment and Recruiting

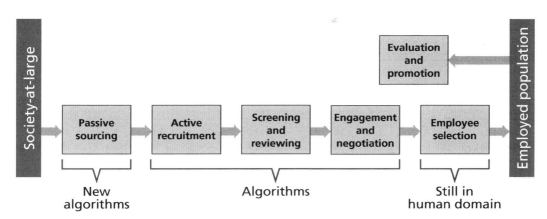

different points where inequity might enter the decisionmaking process. We will focus on two phases of the pipeline: passive sourcing and active recruitment.

Passive Sourcing

Passive sourcing of candidates is a prime example of algorithms and big data being used to create new services that did not previously exist. *Passive sourcing* is the search for *passive candidates*—individuals who work at other companies and are not actively seeking a new job but, based on available data, are open to a new job in the near future.

One company that offers this service, Entelo, claims that it combs through 450 million passive candidates for its clients. It does this through a proprietary metric, called "More Likely to Move," that assesses "dozens of predictive variables." Candidates flagged as likely to move "are twice as likely to move to a new job within the next 90 days" (Entelo, 2018).

As more personal and business data become available online, this type of practice is likely to become more powerful and prominent. Employee "poaching" is already a renowned occurrence in Silicon Valley. By identifying individuals who are not actively seeking a job but could be convinced to switch companies, passive sourcing gives businesses a competitive advantage in attaining the best talent.

Another algorithmic tool to recruit passive candidates is through digital marketing and targeted advertisements in social media, search results, email, or elsewhere online. The use of recruitment ads is a long-used practice, but online platforms now enable employers to purchase ads precisely targeted to specific demographics or psychological profiles, including values, opinions, and interests. There are knotty legal questions about whether employment ads can be targeted based on legally protected categories. After a ProPublica article and an investigation by the Washington state attorney general, Facebook agreed not to allow third-party advertisers to target ads that exclude ethnic groups, religious minority groups, and LGBTQ groups (Angwin and Parris, 2016; Washington State Office of the Attorney General, 2018). Initially this decision applied to housing, credit, and employment advertisements, but it was also expanded to insurance and other types of "public accommodation."

However, Facebook still allowed advertisers to target ads based on age. Facebook and other companies that conduct digital marketing have defended the practice of selling age-based targeted ads, arguing that "age-based targeting for employment purposes is an accepted industry practice and for good reason: it helps employers recruit and people of all ages find work" (Goldman, 2017). Similar arguments have been made about the benefits of the precise targeting of other demographic profiles.

Active Recruitment

To attract applicants to an open position, a business creates a job description and advertisement (a process which can also be automated). After posting the opening, instead of waiting for resumes to be submitted, businesses can review application aggregation websites to identify individuals with the skills they are seeking. They can also revisit previous candidates who were turned down for similar positions. The problem that human recruiters have with this portion of the process is that there are far too many possible qualified candidates for them to select a feasible number to contact directly.

To facilitate active recruitment, employers can use machine learning algorithms for at least three purposes. First, using supervised learning from existing company data, they can identify which types of recruits (or which candidates they previously turned down) most resemble their highest-performing employees (Singh et al., 2010). Because performance evaluation and promotion are also subject to bias on sensitive attributes, feedback loops are generated that perpetuate or magnify structural injustices instead of promoting objectivity or fairness. Second, as with passive recruitment, employers may seek new recruits through online targeted advertising and can refine marketing toward people likely to be seeking new work. Third, recruitment companies can automatically comb third-party websites based on client-specified criteria, including whether individuals have visited the companies' websites or by individuals' geographic location. They can also perform linguistic and personality analysis from social media profiles, such as LinkedIn and Facebook (Faliagka, Tsakalidis, and Tzimas, 2012; Caers and Castelyns, 2011).

As discussed above, it is risky for employers to look at some available candidate information—accessing protected-status data prior to a hiring decision being made can result in a Title VII allegation if the candidate is not hired. A lack of written policy can also result in a discrimination claim if social media searches result in information that does not treat all applicants fairly—it is difficult to prove that, once accessed, the information was not used in a hiring decision. Without written hiring procedures, applicants who were not hired may be able to allege that they were illegally questioned or that information about them was illegally used in a final hiring decision (Maurer, 2018).

However, third parties can still evaluate and scrub social media information. For instance, one organization says it redacts "names, gender, alma maters, and other personal identifiers" before returning resumes to recruiters to remove the risk of recruiters directly seeing that information (Talvista, undated). A different organization has developed flags for sexism, bigotry, crime, and other "company-specific issues" to help filter out individuals with that sort of information present on their social media profiles (Fama, undated). In this way, algorithms provide a way for companies to distance themselves from potential legal liability.

Equity Challenges in Recruitment Algorithms

Despite the claims of recruitment algorithm developers, potentially serious equity risks still exist.

Limited Reach

First, there is concern about whether recruitment algorithms are able to equitably reach the people who are a good fit for the organization. People with greater access to online resources (e.g., people in urban areas as opposed to rural areas) and online security functions (e.g., people with protection programs against identity theft and other online liabilities) will benefit more than those without such advantages. To some extent, this imbalance is unavoidable—it would be an impossible burden to expect employers to identify all qualified candidates that exist in the world every time they want to hire a new employee. However, there are equity concerns when the candidates who are identified are disproportionately chosen based on race, gender, or other sensitive characteristics. For instance, it is more expensive to buy targeted advertising aimed at women than men, which is associated with a larger number of men seeing ads for science careers than women (Fine Maron, 2018). Targeted advertising has also been demonstrated to present more men than women with high-paying jobs (Spice, 2015), discriminate based on age by preferring younger hires (Angwin, Scheiber, and Tobin, 2017), and discriminate based on race (Pager and Pedulla, 2015). In this way, equally qualified members of some groups are excluded from employment opportunities.

Opacity of Validation Criteria

Second, proprietary and opaque algorithms invite a host of questions about how they determine the fitness of a candidate for a position. Are some demographics of equally qualified people more likely to be selected for than others because of unforeseen bias? Without a full list of the variables that are used in such algorithms, as well as auditing to ensure that algorithms are performing as expected, neither businesses using a service nor candidates who are screened by it can verify that their information is being used in an appropriate manner. The variables used may be proxies for blacklisted characteristics, thus inadvertently reinforcing historical biases. Increased transparency about how algorithms are trained, verified, and implemented will improve trust of and oversight into the processes in which they are involved, as would enabling third-party research to corroborate industry-created research and case studies. However, encouraging transparency in privately created algorithms is difficult to balance with the nature of for-profit businesses. Proprietary intellectual capital, such as an algorithm, is closely guarded, yet trade-offs should be made to generate more-universal trust in these decision aids.

Training Data Issues

Third, in recruitment scenarios in which historical data is used to train an algorithm, the biases of previous human recruiters can be translated into digital rules. To determine the "best" employee, the data on past "good" employees will be based on previous hires. Even if hiring practices had not been overtly discriminatory, most previous employees (because of structural inequality with regard to access to education, for instance) may have been white, male, or both. The algorithm will have much more information about this class of people and, therefore, is more likely to make positive classifications on these more available data. This can also occur when companies mine their previous applicant pool for the same type of information. The Amazon case described at the beginning of this chapter is one actual example of this phenomenon.

This concern relates to an overarching question about what precisely constitutes a success criterion for recruitment algorithms, highlighting the competing concepts of equity in employment described earlier with respect to the Civil Rights Act.

Inadequacy of Variable Blacklisting

Fourth, as we have seen, a major legal approach to protecting equity in employment is to identify a set of protected categories that should not factor into employment decisionmaking. Recruitment algorithms can blacklist these variables—but even if protected status information is removed, machine learning algorithms are exceptionally good at identifying proxy variables in big data sets that are correlated with protected categories. For example, geographic indicators are frequently highly correlated with race, even though "address" is not a protected variable (Calders and Žliobaitė, 2013).

Teasing out the differences between a variable that is highly predictive of a successful employee and a variable that is indicative of historical discrimination is not a trivial task. Many of the pieces of information that are considered the most consequential for hiring decisions, such as educational background, years of experience in certain positions, or physical proximity to the position, can be tied to sensitive variables, such as religion, gender, race, and wealth. Without processes for auditing and challenging the decisions made by recruitment algorithms, these biases will be carried forward and potentially exacerbated.

Algorithmic Accountability

Fifth, an accountability gap may exist regarding algorithms. Although algorithms may hedge against legal liability, they can create an accountability gap, as discriminatory practices can still occur without the employer or third-party algorithm provider being directly responsible for these discriminatory practices. The fair hiring laws enforced by the EEOC and essential to the Fair Credit Reporting Act only apply to humans. Legal precedent has not yet caught up with the technical reality of outsourced algorithmic recruitment. Transferring the responsibility of hiring from humans to machines does not eliminate discrimination, it merely shifts the responsibility to a party that is not under legal scrutiny.

Murky Implications for Compliance

Sixth, algorithms complicate the application of antidiscrimination law. As noted above, the burden for showing disparate treatment and disparate impact falls on the plaintiff. Under a standard burden-shifting framework for disparate treatment, the conscious intention to discriminate is essential (*Mcdonnell Douglas Corp. v. Green*, 1973). Yet it is difficult to discern the conscious intention of an algorithm. After all, one cannot overhear an algorithm making disparaging remarks about an individual's race, sexual orientation, or other characteristic. Algorithms without conscious motive would be immune to this test, and no legal framework exists to pursue correction and protection (Barocas and Selbst, 2016). Existing legal norms do not fully capture practical ethical intuitions about inequity.

Implementation Uncertainties

Finally, there are major questions regarding implementation practices. Algorithms are complicated: Can a hiring manager understand them? Do managers have policies in place for proper use? Just as with the COMPAS recidivism algorithm, the use of recruitment tools will vary, as will human trust of these algorithmic recruitment tools. In many cases, recruitment algorithms will be one tool among many, and possible weaknesses will be mitigated by other resources. In other instances, algorithms will do the preponderance of the work, and humans will only make the final hiring decisions—without understanding the data synthesis that went into generating the information they are using.

Effective and thorough implementation of algorithms requires a partnership of understanding between the information and the decisionmakers, and this means acknowledging and highlighting areas in which business practices are not aligned with societal norms of equity and fairness.

Closing Thoughts

Algorithms are already in use at various stages of the recruitment pipeline, and their use will only become more common. We only explore two areas of use in this report, but further data-based possibilities exist for other decision points. All these uses and possibilities have the potential to reduce the amount of bias in hiring—or codify it and make it worse. However, the promise of algorithms is too powerful to ignore: They have the potential to reduce hiring discrimination, promote diversity, and level the playing field, so that candidates are actually judged based on their merits and their fit for the job.

There is still more work to do to make algorithms better tools for reducing bias, accurately reflecting societal norms and legal intent, while ensuring that they are still cheap, fast, and accurate. Advanced practical algorithms did not exist when most of the existing laws to protect against discrimination were designed. The frameworks built by lawmakers do not take into account biases by machines trained on human data and acting without intent to discriminate. Updating these legal frameworks to acknowledge these issues is essential. Part of this process involves humans determining the values and norms that we want algorithms to perpetuate. What mix of fairness, accuracy, and efficiency is best for the most at risk?

The use of algorithms in recruitment complicates many of the questions of compliance with which organizations must contend. For instance, if the hiring organization uses a third party to review the applications it received, and the algorithm uses blacklisted variables, who (or what) is liable for a discriminatory denial of position? If an algorithm ignores blacklisted variables but uses highly correlated proxies, is it violating the intent of the law, if not the letter of it? Conversations at the national policy level with the tech industry, affected protected groups, and hiring bodies are needed to acknowledge and address these issues. Without a transparent and open process, biases will persist, and new ones may arise.

In addition, research into the use of recruitment algorithms is in the beginning stages, and it is remarkably difficult to gain access to the necessary data resources for further inquiries. Proprietary data sets and algorithms make peer-reviewed analysis of processes impossible except by the controlling organization—which promotes neither trust nor progress.

The sorts of questions that should be considered by researchers investigating recruitment algorithms are not just deeply technical. To consider how algorithms are built, used, and maintained, ethics must be incorporated into the research discussion. We provide a starting list of questions that should be considered when scrutinizing recruitment algorithms.

- What assessment can be done to ensure that certain groups do not receive undue benefit or burden from the algorithm?

- Which value(s) does the algorithm pursue—e.g., a more diverse field of candidates? equal treatment of candidates?—and how is it achieving them?
- Which data sets were used to train the algorithm, and how accurately do those data sets represent the population on which the algorithm will be used?
- Does the algorithm access any blacklisted variables, and how does it consider them—as factors to weigh carefully to address historical disadvantages or as ways to exclude at-risk groups from services?
- Who is legally liable for violations if a grievance is expressed: the hiring organization, the third party who built the algorithm, or the algorithm itself?
- How is the algorithm used—as one information aid among many or as the primary source of information in decisionmaking? Which regulations and practices are built around algorithmic use?

Without open data, the ability to examine black-box algorithms, and open conversations about the values we wish to imbue in our AI, the history of inequality in U.S. hiring may continue into the digital age.

CHAPTER FIVE

Domain Exploration: Algorithms in U.S. Criminal Justice Systems

Algorithms are being implemented at every phase of the criminal justice decision pipeline (see Figure 5.1).

One of the most widespread uses of algorithms in the criminal justice system is for risk assessment—e.g., for assessing recidivism and probation violation risks. The use of algorithms for risk assessment has also received the most outside attention. This section focuses on the use of risk assessment within the court phases of the criminal

Figure 5.1
Notional Rendition of Decision Pipeline for the U.S. Criminal Justice System

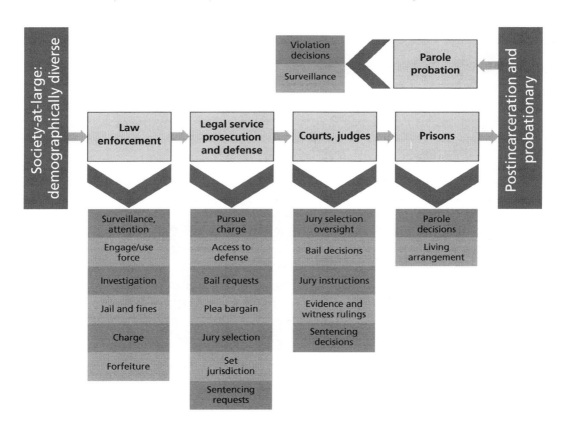

justice pipeline.[1] In this context, risk assessment tools are used to determine pretrial detention decisions, sentencing, treatment and rehabilitation for incarcerated offenders, and parole and probation decisions. These tools were first used for probation decisions, then pretrial decisions, and most recently for sentencing (including some subdecisions about treatment and rehabilitation while incarcerated). The statutes that authorize (and occasionally mandate) the use of these tools vary widely from state to state.

The Criminal Justice Decision Pipeline

Pretrial Detention

Risk-assessment tools are often used for pretrial detention and release decisions and, in this context, generally place more focus on static risk factors. One pretrial tool, the Public Safety Assessment, is used in three states (Arizona, Kentucky, and New Jersey) and dozens of local jurisdictions in other states. The Public Safety Assessment was developed by the Laura and John Arnold Foundation. It was built using data from 1.5 million crimes across 300 U.S. jurisdictions in an attempt to help make decisions about whether an individual should be detained or released before trial, but it is not meant to be used for other considerations (e.g., rehabilitation).

Sentencing

Using algorithmic tools for sentencing is a relatively new development; in 1994, Virginia became the first state to implement a recidivism risk assessment instrument for sentencing decisions (Ostrom et al., 2002). This instrument, created by the Virginia Criminal Sentencing Commission, was designed to divert 25 percent of the lowest-risk offenders to nonprison sanctions. In 1999, Virginia developed a second instrument; this time, the goal was to identify the *highest*-risk offenders. High-risk sex offenders' sentences could be increased as much as threefold (Monahan and Skeem, 2014).

In Utah, although judges maintain discretion in the final sentencing decision, they must consider the recommendation of the Office of Adult Probation and Parole, which involves the use of an assessment of risk and needs. This assessment accounts for such factors as education level, substance abuse, and homelessness (Utah Sentencing Commission, 2012).

Within the justice system, dissent exists regarding the use of risk-assessment instruments in sentencing. Under the rubric of evidence-based sentencing, a draft of

---

[1]   Other uses in the criminal justice pipeline include predictive policing, facial recognition, and probabilistic DNA genotyping and analysis (see Cino, 2018).

the Model Penal Code explicitly endorses the use of these instruments.[2] However, the Department of Justice remarked in 2014 that

> analysis of current risk assessment tools demonstrate that utilizing such tools for determining prison sentences to be served will have a disparate and adverse impact on offenders from poor communities already struggling with many social ills (Wroblewski, 2014).

Using risk assessment tools for sentencing may be more difficult than using them for pretrial and probation decisions, as the goals for pretrial detention, probation, and parole decisions are more straightforward (e.g., maintaining public safety, ensuring that individuals will show up for trial or to meetings with their probation officer). To the extent that risk assessment instruments reflect recidivism risk, the relevance of this score to general deterrence and retribution is questionable. Additionally, pretrial detention and parole are essentially binary decisions, and the parameters of probation are relatively circumscribed. Although there are sentencing guidelines, in most cases, judges have significant discretion in these decisions.

If algorithms are to be used in sentencing, the justice system should consider the various goals of punishment (deterrence, retribution, incapacitation, and rehabilitation), and make explicit what balance of these goals they are trying to achieve. The algorithm could then be maximized to create this desired balance.

Treatment and Rehabilitation

Utah uses the sentencing recommendation scores mentioned earlier to assess which "life skills" classes best meet an inmate's needs and to determine conditions of probation. Newly imprisoned inmates in Pennsylvania are evaluated with the Risk Screening Tool to assess their risk of recidivism. They are categorized into low-, medium-, and high-risk groups. Medium- and high-risk inmates may complete further assessments and possibly must complete a treatment plan addressing their "criminogenic needs" before being considered for parole (Monahan and Skeem, 2014).

Parole and Probation

Rudimentary "algorithms" used for probability-based assessment long predate what we might consider the current algorithmic boom. In the first half of the 20th century, Ernest W. Burgess and others created expectancy tables for parole prediction, which included such factors as work history, marital status, and prison rule violations (Burgess, 1936). In the 1970s, the Salient Factor Score was first developed for use in federal

---

[2]   The Model Penal Code is meant to help standardize penal codes among U.S. states. The text authorizes the sentencing commission to develop instruments that assess offenders' amenability to rehabilitation and risk to public safety, and "[w]hen these instruments or processes prove sufficiently reliable," they may be incorporated into the sentencing guidelines (American Law Institute, 2017, § 6B.09).

parole guidelines; in that era, it was considered unfair to include immutable characteristics (e.g., race, ethnicity, gender, and age) in parole and sentencing criteria (Gottfredson, Wilkins, and Hoffman, 1978; Hoffman, 1983; Tonry, 2013). In 1982, RAND researchers wrote a report on selective incapacitation—the probabilistic analytical trend that was popular in that era (Greenwood and Abrahamse, 1982). Although the focus of the report is explicitly not about "difficult choices among conflicting values," the issues that the report does raise are relatively parallel to issues regarding the use of algorithms in criminal justice today. The report raises questions about the ethics of using certain factors (e.g., marital status, education), if correlated with offense rates, as predictors. It also acknowledged the problem of false positives (offenders incorrectly classified as high-offense-rate criminals) as undermining the presumption of innocence.

Relevant Concepts of Equity in Criminal Justice

Equal protection requires that similarly situated persons are treated alike; disparate treatment may be disallowed. However, most group classifications used in risk/needs assessments are only subject to *rational basis review*, which means that as long as the policy has a legitimate purpose and that the risk-needs assessment is rationally related to that purpose, its constitutionality will be upheld. The two largest—though not the only—exceptions to this are gender, which is subject to *heightened review*, and race, which is subject to *strict scrutiny*. With regard to race, many scholars believe that including race in criminal justice decisions would be unconstitutional; even those who disagree still believe that it would be unseemly (Tonry, 2014).

Although directly including race is problematic, many risk-needs tools have other variables that essentially act as race proxies. Disparate impact could still be observed across race groups, even if the algorithm were supposedly racially neutral; however, statistically significant associations have generally not been sufficient for courts to find discriminatory intent, and thus an equal protection argument based on proxy variables would have an uphill battle.

Due process requires, at minimum, notice and the opportunity for a hearing. This does not always occur; algorithms have cut off people's benefits without warning (Eubanks, 2018), and the algorithm that creates the No-Fly List does not inform individuals of its decisions. Even if notice is provided, an affected person may be unable to remedy the issue because the reasoning for the algorithm's decision is unavailable—either because of trade secret restrictions or because it is technically infeasible. The opportunity for a hearing is perhaps a less obvious problem, but it would likely be difficult for an individual to argue against the decision of a nonhuman device (one cannot examine a computer as an adverse witness). Additionally, automation bias has been shown to exist in many contexts, making it even more difficult for an individual to argue against a machine (Cummings, 2006; Skitka et al., 2000).

Risk prediction for sentencing is often in tension with retributive, utilitarian, and restorative concepts of proportional punishment. Retributive theory requires just punishments to be proportionate, because the punishments express public beliefs about the offender's moral blameworthiness. However, recidivism-risk assessments are not geared toward determining proportionate response to *past* crimes, but rather toward assessing risk based on probability of *future* offenses. Utilitarian theory also arguably requires proportionality to improve future deterrence (e.g., attempts should be punished less severely than completed crimes). Restorative justice also requires proportionality, although not explicitly; while it allows for differing consequences for similar crimes based on victim needs, there is an upper boundary to the proportionate sentence that the justice system would impose.

Equity Challenges

Procedural Justice and Voice

As in our other contexts, what constitutes fairness is a difficult question. Fairness in the law can be measured in terms of outcome or in terms of process. Research on procedural justice suggests that the perceived fairness of the process is more important to people than the outcome (Tyler, 1994). However, the fact of this preference does not entail that it is morally correct. Within the framework of procedural justice, algorithms still impact several distinct equity concerns. For a process to be perceived as procedurally just, an institution should strive for transparency, consistency, neutrality, proportionality, accuracy, and voice (Simmons, 2018; Tyler, 2003; Truxillo, Bauer, and Sanchez, 2001; Dolan et al., 2007).

Voice, in this discussion, refers to mechanisms that enable affected subjects to express their concept of equity, dissent to a decision, or reshape the structure of a decisionmaking process. It is a form of system feedback that is often necessary if an institution is to remain aligned with the values of its subjects. Affected subjects are also more likely to accept the legitimacy of decisionmaking processes in which they have a voice. But providing a voice is difficult to guarantee in a large institution, and minority voices are often not heard.

Opacity

Risk assessment algorithms in common use today fail a primary test because many legal scholars have flagged a lack of transparency as the biggest issue with these algorithms.[3] This opacity impacts the ability of outside observers to assess the algorithm for

---

[3] See Desai and Kroll, 2017 (arguing that transparency is important, but insufficient, and arguing for the technical concept of computer-science accountability to be imported into the law) and Carlson, 2017.

accuracy and bias. It also makes it more difficult for a defendant to challenge the use of the algorithm using an equal protection argument.

Although opacity makes assessing other factors even more difficult, the effects of opacity on evaluations of accuracy and consistency are particularly important issues to address. The effects of opacity on accuracy and consistency evaluations also implicate concerns about bias. Error rates in assessing recidivism may be biased or unbalanced, as some of the COMPAS studies have suggested. However, even if an algorithm is accurate, it may still be biased as a result of the data used to build it; for example, heavier policing in poor and minority neighborhoods may make it appear that these communities commit a higher proportion of crimes than they actually do (Kehl, Guo, and Kessler, 2017).

Normative Clarity

As algorithms continue to increase their presence in justice-system decisionmaking, policymakers must decide which concept(s) of fairness and social justice are most important. Different fairness goals may be incompatible with one another, and policymakers will need to prioritize their aims. Without a clear idea of what kind of fairness the algorithm is trying to achieve, assessing whether it is, in fact, fair is impossible. A specific definition of fairness also allows outsiders to comment and critique the justice system's priorities in this area. In addition to defining important concepts of fairness, policymakers should specifically define the goals of their algorithmic assessments (Skeem and Monahan, 2011).

Audit and Due Process

Another suggestion for addressing some of the fairness issues caused by algorithmic assessments is a specifically defined "technological due process" (Keats Citron, 2008; Keats Citron and Pasquale, 2014). The most important element would be full transparency, including public source code and audit trails. This would improve the "notice" criterion of the due process analysis. This level of transparency may require a public or nonprofit entity to create and maintain the risk assessment algorithm, as companies with proprietary algorithms are unlikely to allow the necessary access. The financial goals of for-profit companies (e.g., for-profit prisons) may be in tension with the fairness required in the justice system.

Combating the issues with the "hearing" prong of the analysis would require confronting automation bias and making clear to hearing officers and judges that automated systems are fallible. Algorithms also need to be validated and periodically revalidated on the local population; certain variables' predictive value may decrease over time.

In the next chapter, we observe a specific example of auditing: the audit of the use of algorithms in the North Carolina criminal justice system. The audit focuses on one decision point in that system (supervision levels in the postincarceration and probation phase). Audits of this type will be necessary to answer equity challenges both today and in the future.

Closing Thoughts

Besides the equity challenges raised in the previous section, there is still the practical concern of how to run an algorithm audit on a system as complex as the criminal justice system. The next chapter demonstrates a limited audit for a subpart of the criminal justice system. Full audits may consist of many such subsystem audits. However, creating fair subsystems may not guarantee fairness within the full system. Issues related to implementation, or evolving or completely new standards of equity, may require a more holistic assessment of the use of algorithms in criminal justice settings.

CHAPTER SIX

Analytic Case Study: Auditing Algorithm Use in North Carolina's Criminal Justice System

In this chapter, we present a proof-of-concept audit of algorithm use in a social application: recidivism risk assessment in the North Carolina criminal justice system. We examine the use of a risk and needs assessment score used by the North Carolina Department of Public Safety, developed and normed on the local population, and describe

- how the algorithm meets various definitions of equity
- how it performs at predicting serious probation violations and the commission of new crimes across races.

Our key finding here is that North Carolina's recidivism risk assessment tool is fairly unbiased with respect to race (in terms of "white" and "black" categories). However, measured race-based differences in "technical violations" suggest further analysis is needed (and ongoing).

This exploration is intended as a concrete minimal illustration of the kinds of important details and questions (including technical questions about relevant statistical measures) that arise in an application audit. It also includes normative details about the standards for procedural justice.

Background

The supervision of adult offenders in North Carolina who are on probation, parole, or post-release supervision is the responsibility of the Division of Adult Correction and Juvenile Justice of the North Carolina Department of Public Safety. Its Division of Community Corrections employs approximately 2,200 people and supervises slightly more than 100,000 offenders.[1] The supervision model adopted by the agency recog-

---

[1]   This includes approximately 8,500 offenders in the Community Service Work Program (North Carolina Department of Public Safety, Division of Adult Correction and Juvenile Justice, Community Corrections, 2018).

nizes that different offenders may require and benefit from different amounts of supervision, using five levels of supervision based on a risk/needs model. To that end, the division implemented a risk-needs assessment. The assessment takes place no later than 60 days after the offender has been placed under supervision (North Carolina Department of Public Safety, Division of Adult Correction and Juvenile Justice, Community Corrections, 2016).

For the *risk assessment,* the division uses an adapted version of the Offender Traits Inventory, a validated tool that scores individuals on a scale of zero to 100.[2] Depending on the resulting Offender Traits Inventory score, offenders are classified into one of five risk levels: extreme (scores 66 and above), high (50 to 65), moderate (26 to 49), low (11 to 25), and minimal (zero to ten). These assessments were created to predict *re-arrest,* not probation performance. The actual instruments are not publicly available, but they include and weigh various aspects of the offender's criminal record and other traits, such as age, employment, and education (Markham, 2012). For the *needs assessment,* the division uses an in-house tool consisting of two worksheets: "Offender Self-Report" and "Officer Interview and Impressions." The tools ask questions that flag "criminogenic needs," which are factors related to criminal behavior. These include association with peers involved in criminal activity, family dysfunction, and substance use. Offenders are then classified into one of five needs levels; again, extreme, high, moderate, low, and minimal. Results from the risk and needs assessments separately are used to place offenders into a five-by-five matrix to determine their supervision level.

Based on information collected during the risk and needs assessments, the system assigns offenders to one of five supervision levels, numbered L1 through L5. Depending on the supervision level, the nature and intensity of the contact between the offender and probation officer changes, as do the applicable responses to offender noncompliance. The relationship between supervision levels and various combinations of risk and needs levels is captured in Table 6.1. Certain types of offenders (e.g., documented gang offenders, domestic violence offenders, sex offenders, some driving while intoxicated offenders) are assigned to a higher supervision level irrespective of the result of their risk and needs assessments.

L1 consists of the most prescriptive supervision requirements and noncompliance sanctions, and is reserved for offenders with the highest risks and needs. By contrast, the lowest, least-restrictive supervision levels are intended for offenders with the lowest risks and needs (see Table 6.2 for supervision levels). Probation officers have the discretion to supervise at a higher level—either officially with the sign off of their supervisor, or unofficially, but it is not clear from the data provided whether this is a common occur-

---

2   Adult male offenders ordered to register as a sex offender are also required to complete the Static-99 risk assessment (North Carolina Department of Public Safety, Division of Adult Correction and Juvenile Justice, Community Corrections, 2016).

Table 6.1
Relationship Between Supervision Levels and Risk/Needs Levels

		Risk Level				
		Extreme	High	Moderate	Low	Minimal
Needs Level	Extreme	L1	L1	L2	L3	L3
	High	L1	L2	L3	L3	L3
	Moderate	L2	L2	L3	L4	L4
	Low	L2	L2	L4	L4	L5
	Minimal	L2	L2	L4	L5	L5

Table 6.2
Supervision Level Minimum Contact Standards

Supervision Level	Contact Standard
Level 1	• One Offender Management Contact every 30 days • One Home Contact every 30 days • One Weekend Home Contact every 60 days
Level 2	• One Offender Management Contact every 30 days • One Home Contact every 60 days • Sex offenders: One Home Contact every 30 days
Level 3	• One Offender Management Contact every 30 days • One Home Contact every 60 days • Sex offenders: One Home Contact every 30 days
Level 4	• One Offender Accountability review every 30 days • One Face-to-Face Contact every 90 days • Verify Financial Management System and special conditions compliance every 30 days • Conduct Home Contact within 30 days to verify change in address
Level 5	• One Offender Accountability review every 30 days • Verify Financial Management System and special conditions compliance every 60 days • Conduct Home Contact within 30 days to verify change in address

SOURCE: North Carolina Department of Public Safety, Division of Adult Correction and Juvenile Justice, Community Corrections, 2016.
NOTES: Offender Management Contact is the primary face-to-face interaction between the offender and the officer. In addition to monitoring compliance and addressing needs, Home Contact is designed to assess the offender's living conditions and elicit support from the offender's household. The Financial Management System is maintained by the Administrative Office of the Courts; however, it is probation officers who are responsible for verifying all supervision fees have been paid.

rence, nor can we report on the factors that probation officers might consider in exercising this discretion.

Assessment of Algorithmic Bias

We examined the predictive validity of the risk assessment score on serious probation violations (including the commission of a new crime, reincarceration, or a serious public safety violation, such as the unlawful possession of a firearm) to test whether the algorithms were equitable in terms of their predictive accuracy. The department provided us with a de-identified file with all individuals over 18 years of age who began a community supervision sentence in 2011–2016, with all information on their probation periods through August 2017.

There were 387,363 total probation spells from 321,880 individuals; for individuals with more than one probation spell, we selected the first one. We narrowed our sample down to the 302,256 cases with at least a one-year follow up (i.e., entered prior to August 2016) and a valid risk assessment score ($n = 231,357$; see Table 6.3). All individuals who changed risk, supervision, or need level during their probation spell were also removed, along with everyone in the sample who was not either black or white (7 percent of the population) or had missing data on other fields. This left a final sample of 198,949. There did not appear to be any differences in the demographic or offense features between our sample and the original 321,880 in the data set.

The client-level information we received included the following categories:

1. **Demographics**: gender, race, ethnicity, age at probation entry
2. **Probation Sentence Information**: county of supervision, type of supervision (probation versus parole), supervision entry and end dates, probation officer
3. **Probation Assessments**: risk score, risk level, needs level, supervision level
4. **Probation Violations**: our dependent measure, which we coded into *serious violations*, e.g., commission of a new crime, public safety violation, and *technical violations*, e.g., failure to appear for an appointment and pay court-ordered fees according to schedule.

Most of the community supervisees were male (72 percent) and either white (55.8 percent) or black (44.2 percent), with an average age of 33 (mean = 33.21, standard deviation = 12.16). They were serving sentences for an average of 1.3 offenses (standard deviation = 0.70), which included property crimes (29 percent), vehicle crimes (28 percent), drug crimes (28 percent), and violent crimes (20 percent); only a few were serving sentences for sex (3 percent) or weapon (3 percent) charges.

On average, the black community supervisees (mean = 33.87, standard deviation = 19.23) scored significantly higher on risk than nonblack supervisees (mean =

Table 6.3
Distribution of Probation Assessment Results by Race (percentage)

	Black $n = 87,979$	White $n = 110,970$	Overall
Risk level			
Extreme	10.7	8.3	9.4
High	18.2	17.4	17.8
Moderate	35.0	32.8	33.8
Low	29.6	33.6	31.7
Minimal	6.5	8.0	7.3
Need level			
Extreme	20.2	22.2	21.3
High	17.2	15.8	16.5
Moderate	36.9	38.8	37.9
Low	21.7	18.8	20.2
Minimal	4.1	4.3	4.2
Supervision			
Level 1	8.5	7.0	7.7
Level 2	28.4	27.7	28.1
Level 3	31.8	33.6	32.7
Level 4	26.9	27.2	27.0
Level 5	4.4	4.5	4.5

28.13, standard deviation = 17.11), t (198947) = -69.34, $p < 0.001$. The distribution of clients to risk, need, and supervision levels differed by race, but by less than 3 percent across each level ($x^2(4)$ = 919.55, p < 0.001; $x^2(4)$ = 213.07, $p < 0.001$; $x^2(4)$ = 261.31, $p < 0.001$, respectively).

Without adjusting for any other differences, we found small differences in the commission of serious violation rates by supervision level and by race (see Table 6.4). These differences could be caused by a difference in the base rate of serious violations/recidivism, performance of the algorithm, offender profiles, or differences in implementation.

Table 6.4
One-Year Violation Rates by Race and by Supervision Level (no controls; percentage)

Supervision Level	Black	Nonblack
Level 1	27.3	25.0
Level 2	20.1	18.2
Level 3	14.1	14.7
Level 4	8.8	8.7
Level 5	4.4	3.9

Next, we ran a series of multivariate logistic models so that we could more precisely isolate the differences in serious violation rates by race (see Table 6.5 for a summary of results). These models controlled for age, gender, offense characteristics, risk score within supervision category, year of entry, county population, and urbanicity. Analyses show that there is a small difference in the commission of a serious probation violation across the supervision categories between black and nonblack probationers. The regression results for race are reported using odds ratios, which are transformations of the coefficients from the logistic regressions. The odds ratios represent the racial disparities between black and nonblack probationers in the different type of violations within each of the supervision categories. The odds ratio for a dichotomous variable should be interpreted as follows: A number over 1 means that this characteristic is positively related to race (black = 1, nonblack = 0)—in other words, an odds ratio higher than 1 means that black probationers are 1.5 times more likely to violate than nonblack probationers, and an odds ratio lower than 1 means that that being black is related to a decrease in odds of that particular outcome.

Overall, black probationers were 3 percent less likely to commit a new crime during their first year of community supervision than nonblacks, controlling for age, gender, offense characteristics, year of entry, and county-level characteristics. However, within supervision categories, there was no difference in four of the five categories. Black probationers were 9 percent less likely to commit a serious probation violation than their nonblack probationer peers in the middle supervision category only.

These analyses suggest that the algorithms that were normed on the local population

1. did not result in large differences in risk or need scores across races
2. did not result in large differences in supervision classification across races
3. did not overestimate or underestimate the serious violation rates between races—meaning that estimation was equally accurate.

It is impossible to say whether this is due to North Carolina following best practices for creating its risk assessments or because of other factors, such as differences in the offending population, definitions of "recidivism," or supervision policies, to name just a few.

Table 6.5
Summary of Multivariate Logistic Regression Results—Odds Ratio

Outcome	L1	L2	L3	L4	L5	Overall
1-year serious probation violation	1.034	0.990	0.911*	1.001	1.088	0.971*

* $p < 0.05$. Full regression results available in Appendix A.

However, when we examine *technical violations*, which are low-level violations that do not constitute the commission of a new crime (such as a failure to appear for a meeting or pay a court-ordered fine according to schedule), a large discrepancy between black and nonblack probationers (54.6 percent versus 43.1 percent) appears. This could be because the black probationer population commits more technical violations or because probation officers are more likely to observe and record these violations. The difference in the technical violation rate is beyond the scope of this project, but since there is no difference in serious violation rates, it does provide preliminary evidence that there may be some bias in these lower-level violations. Therefore, the *bias in the implementation of this algorithm in practice needs further investigation.*

Summary of Audit Analysis

In the next chapter, we provide recommendations for algorithmic best practices. Although the North Carolina algorithm may meet some definitions of equity (e.g., accuracy, equal treatment), in other ways, it does not satisfy some of the criteria in our recommendations.

Specifically, North Carolina's algorithm may not have an appropriate ground truth accuracy criterion. Although the algorithm may be accurate at predicting re-arrest risk, this accuracy is based on past inequitable practices (e.g., differential arrest rates for different races). North Carolina chose re-arrest as its outcome (rather than revocation of probation, a subsequent conviction, or other potential measures); is this the best outcome to choose? It is difficult to determine, as the state did not declare which, if any, normative goals it was trying to improve through the algorithm. As discussed throughout this report, many equity norms are in tension with one another, so it is important to design an algorithm that addresses the ones the state thinks are most important.

Additionally, North Carolina's algorithm is a *black box*—in other words, probationers may know that when they fill out paperwork, it goes "into a computer," but they do not know how their information is used or processed. This impedes procedural equity for the probationers.

CHAPTER SEVEN

Insights and Recommendations

The domain-specific explorations of the previous chapters suggest a range of issues around equity in the use of algorithms. In this concluding chapter, we offer insights gleaned from these cases and make recommendations for addressing equity concerns in the institutional use of algorithms.

Insights from Domain Explorations

1. Equity Is a Contested Concept

There are often multiple reasonable ways to define what is equitable in social institutions. Seemingly reasonable concepts of equity can and do conflict in practice. Conflicting concepts of equity complicate assessment of equity across stakeholders and make it difficult to identify appropriate redress when there are challenges. Even the codified equity norms in specific institutional applications—such as disparate treatment and disparate impact in employment contexts—can at times seem incompatible and require complex interpretation.

This contestation or incompatibility is a specific incarnation of value pluralism (Berlin, 2000). Excessive value pluralism within institutions can be crippling. However, legitimate institutions can expect an *overlapping consensus* among stakeholders that enables institutions to function without full agreement on values (Rawls, 2009, p. 388). Some common ground among key equity concepts is important for working within institutional structures to foster equity across stakeholders.

We examined differing concepts of equity in the sectors of insurance, employment, and criminal justice. These examinations highlight the need to be precise about relevant normative equity criteria in specific applications. It is important to be aware of the plural competing concepts and any required trade-offs between efficiency and fairness.

From a more-concrete mathematical perspective, recent work shows that it is *impossible* to satisfy multiple normatively justifiable concepts of algorithmic fairness (Chouldechova, 2017; Kleinberg, Mullainathan, and Raghavan, 2016; Berk et al., 2017b). The basic perspective on this is that there tends to be a trade-off between efficiency (e.g. predictive accuracy) and fairness (Kleinberg, Mullainathan, and Raghavan, 2016). These impossibility results may motivate a perspective that frames the selection of the governing equity principles as a social choice problem that requires aggregating preferences and choosing the principles most supported. But even this approach runs into restrictions on aggregate or social decisionmaking based on a series of impossibility theorems discovered in the mid-20th century (Arrow, 2012; Gibbard, 1973).

2. Prohibiting Sensitive Attributes Is Less Effective Given Advanced Algorithms and Large Secondary Data Sets

Legal processes for addressing equity in institutional decisionmaking often mandate that certain sensitive attributes not be considered in the decisionmaking process—an approach codified in disparate treatment doctrine. The decisionmaker is obliged to ignore specific identified protected attributes—those considered morally irrelevant to the decision or that reflect past historical injustice. Typical attributes in question include sensitive attributes, such as race, gender, sexual orientation, and *strong correlates thereof* (which may not share the same protection under the law).

There is also some variation on which protected categories are legally or intuitively deemed acceptable in different institutional applications. For example, gender and age are legally, and for many people ethically, permitted as a factor in criminal risk assessment algorithms or insurance algorithms, even though they are generally protected in employment contexts. This underscores the diverse normative landscape across different social applications. Other attributes, such as race, are protected across all of the institutional applications considered here. In this way, sensitive attribute blacklisting is a significant legal approach to promoting equity in otherwise different social applications.

However, the advent of powerful algorithmic decisionmaking artifacts and the proliferation of easily correlative data streams have eroded the power of sensitive-attribute blacklisting to promote equitable outcomes. Data-driven tools now enable the discovery of insensitive secondary data sources and signals that convey information about sensitive attribute status using nonsensitive data sources.[1]

The distinction between functional and statistical independence in decisionmaking lies at the center of this theme. Functional independence encodes our common-sense understanding of independence, as a decision outcome does not take blacklisted variables into account. Statistical independence encodes a perhaps more fairness-relevant understanding of independence: The likelihood of any decision outcome is unrelated to one's sensitive attributes. It is possible to guarantee statistical independence on small decision models by enforcing functional independence; this is traditionally how dispa-

---

[1]   For example, repeated watching of a television station in a specific language might indicate membership in a specific ethnic or racial category. The discovery of similar signals with high *exclusivity indices* can be lucrative for advertising or marketing.

rate treatment doctrine has sought to protect equity. However, it is infeasible to guarantee statistical independence via functional independence on the larger data-driven algorithmic decision models that increasingly dominate. This is because algorithmic models can easily identify and leverage strong correlates of any blacklisted attributes in the larger set of available variables.

The challenges to blacklisting presented by algorithms place additional emphasis on disparate impact analysis as a key component of ensuring equity. As discussed in the case of employment, disparate impact is itself challenging to demonstrate, especially when algorithms are used. Further, disparate impact is generally only observable after an inequitable practice has been in operation for significant time. Alternative methods of mitigating disparate impact and protecting equity in other ways will need to be developed.

3. Ground Truth Accuracy Criteria May Be Inadequate

Most algorithm use cases are evaluated on the basis of their *ground truth accuracy*: how well the model output accurately reflects the true signal the model aims to predict or estimate. For example, risk prediction tools in auto insurance seek to identify facts about genuine risk signals and in criminal justice seek to identify facts about criminal propensities. Similarly, the goal of employment recruitment algorithms is to recruit candidates that are in fact the best fit for the open positions and will thrive in the organization. This ground truth accuracy criterion for the use of algorithms raises three major questions:

1. What happens when it is impossible to observe enough ground truth data to fully calibrate accuracy? This is a common scenario in predictive policing and profiling applications. The same is true for employment, in which it might ultimately be unknown or undecided who precisely is the best for open positions, and there is no way to identify who precisely has been filtered out. True data and false positives are observable, but false negatives go wholly unobserved. Failure to properly account for this observation quirk can lead to runaway feedback loops that amplify discriminatory outcomes. Proper calibration requires algorithmic ingenuity to account for unobserved data (Ensign et al., 2018).[2]

2. What if the available historical data for assessing ground truth is the result of past discriminatory decisionmaking? For instance, the recidivism risk rate that the COMPAS assessment claims to accurately assess is actually the arrest rate—and this rate is arguably based on past and current inequitable practices (such as inequities in surveillance and police attention). Similar questions about the criteria for assessing ground truth might be raised in the insurance and employ-

---

[2] This includes latent variable statistical estimation routines (Ganchev et al., 2009).

ment sectors, in which past discrimination has clearly affected perceptions of risk, as well as employment opportunity.

3. What if the measurement target for ground truth is the wrong one for the application? The use of algorithms in recruitment can easily focus on highlighting candidates comparable to the preexisting pool of "good" current employees. This is an imperfect proxy for candidate fit. In the insurance domain, if the accepted goal is to protect the entire population from extreme events, then accurate risk prediction may be secondary to other social adequacy criteria (e.g., affordability, universal coverage, etc.).

4. Algorithmic Transparency Is Important, But Is Not a Panacea

There is an oft-discussed "explainability" problem with algorithms—algorithms reach conclusions in ways different than humans and are not capable of being probed for human-accessible explanations. This explanatory opacity is sometimes intrinsic to information processing technology; e.g., there are still some technical limits on the interpretability of deep learning models. But explanatory opacity can also be caused by nontechnical factors, such as trade secrecy, copyrights, or just ignorance. All social applications face the challenge of black-box algorithms,[3] but this challenge is particularly acute in contexts in which the opacity of the algorithm raises due process or other procedural equity concerns. In these contexts, the institutions leveraging algorithms might not be able to justify their decisions to affected people, thereby raising persistent doubts about the equity of their decisions.

An additional complication is the role of third-party algorithm developers. Some developers assert intellectual property rights to protect their proprietary models. These intellectual property protections are often in the form of trade secrets protection, creating an accountability conundrum for institutions that deploy proprietary models. The institution relies on the performance of the proprietary model, but it cannot vouch for the acceptability of the model's internal processes. There is an expectation of some degree of transparency about how decisions are made, especially for public sector uses. In the criminal justice context, some legal scholars argue that the use of expert models protected by trade secrecy in judicial decisions effectively constitutes a form of *evidentiary privilege* that is harmful and ahistorical (Wexler, 2018). At a minimum, a degree of transparency enables the possibility of dissent or recourse for inequitable decisions. Yet restrictions on using proprietary systems are still not a widespread norm, and proprietary models are not required to provide transparency about the algorithmic systems they use (Reisman et al., 2018).

---

[3]   It is not necessarily the case that algorithms in our three domains of explorations are intrinsically technically opaque. The insurance industry has a long history of using "linear models" that are particularly easy to explain to regulators, and groups (e.g., Civicscape) are working on transparent recidivism risk estimation algorithms.

Complete algorithmic transparency (if it is even possible) comes with its own risks. Public sector processes might require a measure of secrecy for smooth performance. Basic examples might be the use of operational secrecy for profiling or credit scoring to prevent manipulation from adversarial subjects.[4]

5. Implementation Practices Matter

In the three case studies we discuss, algorithms provide information—about insurance risk, employee quality, and recidivism risk—so humans can make more-informed decisions. In these cases, algorithms are embedded in broader social institutions for a specific purpose, but a human operates as the decisionmaker.

As a result, the broader institutional context of algorithms is important for assessing algorithmic equity. Ultimately, equity is a system-level property encompassing broader dynamics beyond the algorithm. Models of institutions show that it is possible to have inequitable system-level behavior, even when the sublevel algorithms within seem equitable (Ensign et al., 2018).

A variety of human-controlled factors will affect where and how the algorithm is used in a social application. End users will need to understand the benefits and limitations of algorithms to be sure they are using algorithms as intended and to mitigate risks of automation bias or other misuses. The complex nature of algorithms and their relative novelty might lead to confusion without sufficient user training, clear delineations of legal responsibilities, and clear institutional procedures to guide use.

Recommendations and Useful Frameworks

Accuracy, efficiency, and consistency (among other factors) will continue to foster the use of algorithms in decisionmaking within key private and public sector applications, regardless of existing or new equity challenges. There is value in having built-in institutional processes that foster conscious examination of algorithmic equity concerns during design and deployment cycles, not just as an afterthought.

Integrating equity into design is important because these algorithms have the potential to exert significant influence on the lives of their subjects. As a basic framing scheme, it may be useful to view the use of algorithms in social applications (especially high-impact applications) in the same way we view research involving human subjects. The goal of the framing is to foster some *conservatism* in the design and deployment of algorithmic decisionmaking by requiring explicit careful thought about downstream

---

[4]   We can make a (hopefully) useful distinction between *procedural* and *operational* transparency. Procedural transparency refers to the disclosure of the process details underlying a given decision (e.g., release details about the model). Operational transparency refers to the disclosure of all the particular details underlying a given decision (e.g., release the model itself and all available data).

consequences. The Belmont report highlights three principles that should guide human subjects research. These can be adapted for algorithmic decisionmaking.

- **Beneficence**: This requires the intervention to "do no harm." Given the nonlinear responses of decision pipelines, we may construe this to mean "do no *foreseeable* harm."
- **Justice**: This principle requires designers and deployers to think carefully about the distribution of burdens and benefits resulting from the use of their deployed systems. It also suggests that unavoidably harmed users may be entitled to compensation and redress.
- **Respect for personal autonomy**: This principle requires that individuals be treated as autonomous agents. In the context of algorithms, this would include guaranteed rights to notice, consent, and dissent (National Commission for the Protection of Human Subjects of Biomedical and Behavioral Research, 1979).

An institutional focus on these principles in the use of algorithms can provide overarching guidance for more-specific institutional and technical requirements. AI researchers, policymakers, affected persons, and other institutional stakeholders can promote the adoption of these principles as an overall starting point for governance across applications.

This basic overarching framing is not concrete enough to resolve equity challenges in all the varied uses of algorithms. So we make some more-pointed recommendations; first to address the insights drawn from the domain explorations, then to address issues around the technology design and governance processes.

Recommendations in Response to Insights
1. Clarity on Concepts of Equity

We have underscored the issue of normative pluralism and the potential inherent conflicts among concepts of equity. Many applications operate on governing norms negotiated over time, especially when explicit founding contracts are absent. Given the variation in users' moral intuitions, it is safe to assume that there will be uncertainty about and contestation over governing norms.

A measure of *normative clarity* is valuable given this normative uncertainty. Institutions and deployers of algorithmic decisionmaking artifacts need to be clear and transparent about the standards and norms to which they hold themselves. This may include concrete descriptions of why and how institutions use algorithms and the criteria under which an algorithm will be assessed for equity. These statements should also include some explanation of how institutions will respond in cases of competing concepts of equity, or under which conditions other values, such as privacy, interpretability, or efficiency, take precedence. Normative clarity sets clear expectations for users. It also helps prevent costly disappointments or user backlash, as happened with COMPAS.

It is also important to engage stakeholders to ensure that the full range of relevant values is considered. Articulated institutional principles should not be considered infallible or eternal. There is a need to build in opportunities for decision subjects or affected parties to dissent or *voice* competing values. And institutions should strive to address these views and be prepared to undertake reforms.

2. Rely Less on Sensitive Attribute Designation for Assuring Equity

Regulators and institutions may need to be more skeptical about the effectiveness of using attribute blacklists to assure equity. If modern algorithms are increasingly able to find secondary correlates or proxies of sensitive attributes, then institutions will need to consider other ways of achieving equity goals besides simply blinding themselves to a set of specific variables.

Requiring explainable, or even transparent, models may be a better regulatory mechanism for assuring equity. Acceptable explanations will need to demonstrate the relevance of the input signals used for the specific application of the algorithm. For example, a risk estimation model may be required to use only inputs that can reasonably argued to be related to risk.[5]

3. Ground Truth Determinations

Ground truth accuracy may not always be a neutral success condition for judging decisionmaking models. Both algorithm designers and deploying institutions need to think carefully about what outcome they intend to optimize via the use of algorithmic decision aids. They also need to clarify what are acceptable measures of error. This is especially important for applications where there are asymmetric costs associated with false negative and false positive errors (cost-sensitive decisionmaking). They then need to verify that they have the right data needed to train and *evaluate* their algorithmic models.

Clarity on what constitutes ground truth is not always available, and there are decision scenarios (e.g., many profiling use cases) in which full relevant data is not directly accessible.

4. Trustworthy Verification and Validation

The demand for algorithmic transparency is, at its core, a demand for accountability or reliable *warrants of trust* for deployed models. Signals of trustworthiness have to be appropriate to the institutional context and relevant stakeholders. Designing mechanisms for signaling trustworthiness is not always as straightforward as just "opening

---

[5]   California's Proposition 103 establishes a related requirement for auto insurance pricing in the state of California. The measure goes further by imposing a priority order on select risk-relevant factors (e.g., age, gender, driving record). Contributions from other less-obviously risk-relevant factors are capped.

the black box," although it is certainly appropriate for some applications. Opening the black box requires the observer to have the capacity to make useful sense of the disclosed information. Black box audits are not useful without an explanatory frame; they might not ultimately help stakeholders understand how they have been affected. Therefore, they are not always justified, given the complexity of these algorithmic artifacts.

Engineering fields have addressed this verification and validation issue in the past using a variety of mechanisms including, but not limited to, full disclosure to and evaluation by qualified professionals and certificates of compliance issued by professional standards bodies. Other models for assuring trust in social applications might include insurance schemes and tort law to establish clearer attribution of responsibility or culpability.

5. Voice and Human-Aware Implementation

Institutions deploying algorithms should put procedures in place to monitor or evaluate the response to algorithmic decisionmaking artifacts, not just the performance of these artifacts. They should pay attention to how human users react to algorithmic artifacts. This involves giving users more *voice* in the design and deployment process. A bias toward human oversight may be instrumental at mitigating equity concerns in the long run. Implementation guidelines should be transparent outside the institution. This can foster a broader understanding among stakeholders, help set more reasonable user expectations, and enable *dissent* in cases where uses of algorithms are not in compliance with stated practices.

There might be limits to transparency (e.g., privacy reasons, national security), but a bias toward more algorithmic transparency can be instrumental both for improving user trust and for identifying problems quickly. Algorithmic transparency includes transparency about models—including training data—and about usage guidance or limitations.

Institutions may also need to be careful about leveraging third-party purveyors of algorithms. This can create a principal-agent dynamic, in which the third-party agents have incentives and values that are at odds with the contracting institution's values. The agency costs incurred are especially dangerous if there are no audit procedures in place to ensure that third-party solutions align with institutional values. At a minimum, public institutions should set standards or requirements regarding the use of third-party platforms. Institutions should also develop in-house expertise about algorithms and not rely purely on third-party developers.

Technical Recommendations

Designers and deployers of algorithms may benefit from adopting an *algorithmic equity checklist* approach to minimize undesirable equity outcomes. This approach originates from the literature on behavioral interventions to prevent costly mistakes in the field of medical surgery. A systematic review finds that simple basic surgery checklists improve overall safety outcomes (Borchard et al., 2012). Minimal requirements for such a checklist in algorithm development might include the following:

- **Data audits**: Do the training data adequately represent the general population on which the model will be used?[6] Are the training data available for researchers?
- **Model disclosures**: Which relevant model metrics need to be disclosed (besides overall predictive accuracy)? How are accuracy and error estimated? What are the group-specific accuracy and error rates? Does the model use explicit training adaptations to handle data imbalances? Is the model (or *informative* characterizations thereof) publicly accessible in a common format? Is the training code available?
- **Post hoc analyses**: Have model developers characterized the model's sensitivity to the relevant fairness constraints? What is the steepness of any trade-off between enforcing efficiency and fairness (Dickerson, Procaccia, and Sandholm, 2014; Bertsimas, Farias, and Trichakis, 2011; Berk et al., 2017b)? Have algorithmic impact assessments been conducted? How do algorithmic errors propagate through the decision pipeline? Do the users and subjects of the algorithm trust the model? Are users able to extract meaningful explanations for the outcomes of the model?

Our audit case study in the previous chapter gives an example of a post hoc analysis of the use of algorithms in a social application (recidivism risk estimation in criminal justice).

Some elements of this checklist (see Table 7.1) assume little to no intellectual property restrictions on the algorithmic models or training data. Intellectual property restrictions would render some steps difficult or impossible. This assumption is far from a settled norm, and strong admissible business and operational reasons exist for keeping algorithmic models private. However, some legal scholars have identified negative externalities resulting from assertions of intellectual property restriction in the public-sector use of algorithms or in the development of algorithmic models (Wexler, 2018; Levendowski, 2018). The level of transparency (for data and models) may be subject to deliberation in the purpose review step.

Algorithmic Governance

The technical discussion addresses equity from the ground up. Interventions in governance and regulation may be useful for imposing some top-down influence. We use the term *algorithmic governance* to refer to mechanisms that seek to ensure that algorithm use aligns with equity and other public welfare goals. Algorithmic governance

---

[6] This is the *proxy population mismatch* problem that plagues many predictive models based on unrepresentative social media data (Ruths and Pfeffer, 2014).

Table 7.1
Notional Basic Checklist for Algorithmic Equity

Step	Questions	Relevant Tools
Step 0 Purpose review	• Have independent parties vetted the proposed model for downstream consequences? • Is the prediction question the proposed model would solve unobjectionable to the users? • Is the ground truth accuracy criterion both appropriate for the modeling task and socially acceptable?	• Institutional review boards • Human-subjects protection committees • Surveys of affected subjects
Step 1 Data audit	• Do the training data represent the general population on which the model will be used? • Are the training data available for researchers? • Are data sets kept securely and privately?	• Data repositories • Data set summaries • Census demographic statistics • Projected user-base demographic analyses
Step 2 Model audit	• What relevant model metrics need to be disclosed (besides overall predictive accuracy)? • What are the group-specific accuracy and error rates? • Does the model use explicit training adaptations to handle data imbalances? • Is the model (or informative characterizations thereof) publicly accessible in a common format? • Is the training code available? • Can an adversary recover sensitive user data using just access to the model?	• Code repositories (e.g., GitHub)
Step 3 Post hoc analyses	• Have you evaluated the model on the relevant subdemographics in the application? (disaggregated evaluation) • Has the model's price of fairness been characterized? • Have algorithmic impact assessments been conducted? • What are the limitations on the model? • How are mistreated users going to be compensated? Are there avenues for complaint/dissent? • Are users able to extract meaningful explanations for the outcomes of the model? • What secondary uses can the model serve? Are these acceptable? • How do algorithmic errors propagate through implementation or decision pipelines? • Can the use of this model create feedback loops that amplify preexisting inequities?	• Human expert elicitation • User surveys • "Model Cards"[a]

[a] Mitchell et al., 2019.

mechanisms may include regulation, incentive structures, voluntary standards, and other levers.

There are several caveats. Top-down regulation of technology is rife with difficulties. The first difficulty is that traditional regulatory mechanisms are often too slow to keep up with the public welfare concerns posed by rapidly advancing tech innovation. The second common caveat is that heavy-handed or excessive regulation (and its attendant enforceability mechanisms) can stymie tech innovation and impose unmanageable costs. Innovation is an important driver of economic growth and welfare improvements. The goal is to identify flexible, agile regulatory mechanisms to achieve the public good of fair algorithms, especially in public institutions. Any approach must take into account the complexities and nuance of the relevant institution, so effective algorithmic governance may need to be specified at the domain level. The diversity of stakeholders, the complexities of effective governance, and the range of algorithm applications mean that a patchwork of governance regimes might emerge.

"Hard" Governance

There are a variety of governance mechanisms that might be pursued to address the equity issues algorithms present. These mechanisms can exist at various policy levels, including local, state, national, or even supranational (such as the European Union [EU]). Mechanisms codified in government policy are sometimes referred to as *hard governance*. Examples include the EU's General Data Protection Regulation (GDPR), which has been in effect since May 2018, and the state of California's Consumer Privacy Act, which will become law in 2020. These two "hard" mechanisms address algorithmic equity by requiring transparency for data subjects about the data that are collected and how they are used, as well as by giving subjects the right to have their data erased (Regulation [EU] 2016/679, 2016; California Civil Code, 2018).

These features can enable research and testing that can identify equity issues and enable affected people to challenge algorithmic decisions. However, neither of these regulations were established with a specific focus on encouraging equity, and whether the additional transparency promised by these policies actually assists stakeholders in identifying problems and enabling redress is uncertain. In addition, they are not sufficiently fine-tuned to deal with the complexities of different institutional uses of algorithms, so other governance regimes must also be explored.

"Soft" Governance

Other governance mechanisms might be driven by bottom-up coordination among stakeholders on best practices and norms for equitable use—sometimes known as *soft governance* (Marchant and Wallach, 2015). An example is the "Toronto Declaration," which uses the framework of international human rights law to promote the rights to equality and nondiscrimination in machine learning systems and seeks to build agreement on the due diligence responsibilities of private-sector developers and end users of algorithms (Amnesty International and Access Now, 2018). Another example is the "Asilomar AI Principles," which include a judicial transparency provision that has implications for addressing algorithmic equity (Future of Life Institute, undated).[7] Each of these examples were driven by AI researchers and civil-society organizations (e.g., the Institute of Electrical and Electronics Engineers' "Ethically Aligned Design" Standards for AI systems [Institute of Electrical and Electronics Engineers, undated], the Association for the Advancement of Artificial Intelligence standards, or the AI Now recommendations). Soft governance regimes have the advantage of flexibility and potentially greater and more diverse stakeholder engagement (more voice) but lack the punitive or oversight measures that ensure compliance. Without top-down enforcement, soft-governance regimes might be easily overridden or ignored in the challenging cases of algorithmic decisionmaking.

Scope of Operating Mechanisms

The authority level at which a governance mechanism operates is one consideration. Another is the breadth or scope of algorithmic applications a governance mechanism affects. Regulatory frameworks could apply to all entities that use algorithms for decisions, only public agencies that use them, only regulated industries, or some other criterion that distinguishes the use of algorithms in specific applications. Some regimes might apply stricter regulation to institutions that have particular importance or where algorithms impact a large number of stakeholders. For example, Finland has recently established a ban on "discriminating statistical profiling" in the narrow case of financial credit ("Discrimination Through Artificial Intelligence Banned," 2018). California's Consumer Privacy Act applies to all large businesses that collect California residents' data, as determined by the number of persons whose data they collect or the annual revenue of the business (California Consumer Privacy Act, 2018). The GDPR applies to entities that process EU subjects' personal data, but excludes "competent authorities" in criminal justice or national security (Regulation [EU] 2016/679, 2016).

Even in cases where hard regimes have narrow applicability, economic benefits potentially encourage entities to implement the rules in contexts beyond the policy's explicit scope. For example, even though the GDPR only applies to EU subjects, several multinational companies (including Microsoft) have stated that they would extend the regulation's data subject protections to all customers, although the extent of these companies, implementation of these protections remains unclear (Microsoft, 2018).

Table 7.2 identifies a range of governance options for algorithms.

Regulator-Actor Games

We can highlight a theoretical model for agile regulation inspired by insurance regulation in some states: the *regulator-actor game*. This framework for regulation may be useful for thinking about the regulation of fast-paced technologies, such as algorithms and AI. In a regulator-actor game, regulators identify a set of public welfare dimensions

---

[7]   These principles have been endorsed by California (Future of Life Institute, 2018).

Table 7.2
A Range of Governance Options for Algorithms

Governance Scope	Examples	Affected Entities
States	California Consumer Privacy Act	All institutions that use algorithms
Federal	Finnish law	Public institutions that use algorithms
Supranational	GDPR	Regulated industries (insurance, employment)
Industry-led	Toronto Declaration, Asilomar Declaration, Institute of Electrical and Electronics Engineers standards	nonbinding

they intend to promote. Regulators also act as a *proactive* collector of and representative for public concerns (including equity). Competitive private-sector actors then offer public services with or without the use of algorithms while under regular observation or auditing from regulators. Actors also have the responsibility to resolve any equity challenges that regulators identify using any means at their disposal (within reason). This model has the desirable effect of dividing responsibilities: Regulators are responsible for representing public values, and actors are responsible for satisfactory implementation of the value contract the regulators present. A clear division of responsibility can give the public more assurance that their concerns are addressed, and private-sector actors get more clarity on what dimensions their services are being judged for compliance.

Closing Remarks

We have described some of the applications of algorithmic decisionmaking aids in institutions, highlighted a range of risks to equity in these applications, and offered recommendations to provide more accountability, transparency, and deliberation in algorithm use. Future work must focus on developing appropriate governance mechanisms to incentivize institutions to use algorithms responsibly. Different stakeholders—including algorithm developers, deployers, and users—will have different roles in mitigating risks. There is further work to do to identify clear, explicit levers of change available to different stakeholders to prevent equity challenges caused by algorithm use.

We need to remember that a narrow focus on bettering algorithmic decisionmaking aids will not be enough to foster equity. Equity failures in important institutions are longstanding. They are broader and more complex than the mere use of algorithms. Such issues as underresourced public institutions, historical and structural inequality, and injustice present huge difficulties that even perfectly equitable algorithms may not be able to fix.

Algorithms have tremendous potential for improving diverse aspects of society, and the eagerness of our institutions to reap their benefits means that our reliance on them will only continue to grow. As institutions rely more on algorithms, preexisting institutional inequities can easily be reinforced, and new normative concerns may arise. Therefore, it is imperative we develop a deeper, clearer understanding of the risks this trend poses to equity and other institutional values.

Supplemental Tables

This appendix provides complete regression results for the multivariate logistic models described in Chapter Six. Results for the black population are highlighted in bold.

Variable	Highest Supervision		High Supervision		Moderate Supervision		Lower Supervision		Minimal Supervision		Overall	
	b	SE	b	SE	b	SE	b	SE	b	SE	b	SE
Black	**0.033**	**0.042**	**−0.002**	**0.024**	**−0.091**	**0.024**	**−0.008**	**0.033**	**0.091**	**0.114**	**−0.029**	**0.014**
Male	0.101	0.065	0.081	0.032	0.059	0.028	−0.021	0.037	−0.089	0.133	0.054	0.017
Age	−0.019	0.002	−0.021	0.001	−0.020	0.001	−0.019	0.001	−0.015	0.005	−0.021	0.001
Violent Crime	0.076	0.052	0.212	0.032	0.152	0.033	0.095	0.049	−0.209	0.174	0.112	0.018
Property Crime	0.162	0.049	0.172	0.029	0.166	0.030	0.047	0.041	−0.505	0.140	0.085	0.016
Drug Crime	0.040	0.052	−0.001	0.030	0.040	0.031	−0.093	0.041	−0.155	0.152	−0.043	0.017
Sex Crime	−0.041	0.142	−0.309	0.090	−0.642	0.088	−0.351	0.193	−0.450	0.598	−0.412	0.053
Weapon Crime	0.005	0.082	−0.037	0.056	−0.109	0.069	−0.169	0.102	−1.325	0.725	−0.119	0.035
# Charges	0.101	0.020	0.183	0.013	0.340	0.015	0.494	0.022	0.663	0.084	0.276	0.008
2011 Cohort	−0.356	0.214	−0.335	0.160	0.263	0.164	−0.376	0.323	0.744	0.778	−0.128	0.093
2012 Cohort	0.345	0.077	0.371	0.045	0.336	0.047	0.391	0.066	0.695	0.251	0.362	0.026
2013 Cohort	0.281	0.076	0.303	0.044	0.295	0.046	0.337	0.065	0.633	0.251	0.306	0.026
2014 Cohort	0.203	0.078	0.225	0.045	0.154	0.048	0.321	0.066	0.470	0.259	0.215	0.026
2015 Cohort	0.089	0.080	0.159	0.046	0.187	0.048	0.265	0.068	0.400	0.267	0.180	0.027

Variable	Highest Supervision		High Supervision		Moderate Supervision		Lower Supervision		Minimal Supervision		Overall	
	b	SE	b	SE	b	SE	b	SE	b	SE	b	SE
Risk Score	0.012	0.001	0.013	0.001	0.018	0.001	0.022	0.002	0.049	0.012	0.022	0
Population	0	0	0	0	0	0	0	0	0	0	0	0
Rural/Urban	−0.002	0.013	−0.009	0.008	−0.012	0.008	−0.023	0.011	−0.019	0.038	−0.012	0.004
Constant	−1.706	0.140	−1.936	0.071	−2.352	0.074	−2.944	0.099	−4.096	0.391	−2.453	0.040

References

Actuarial Standards Board, *Actuarial Standard of Practice No. 12: Risk Classification (for All Practice Areas), Revised Edition*, Document Number 132, May 1, 2011. As of May 1, 2019:
http://www.actuarialstandardsboard.org/wp-content/uploads/2014/02/asop012_132.pdf

Ajunwa, Ifeoma, Sorelle Friedler, Carlos E. Scheidegger, and Suresh Venkatasubramanian, "Hiring by Algorithm," *Data and Society*, March 10, 2016. As of May 8, 2019:
https://datasociety.net/output/hiring-by-algorithm

Alsever, Jennifer, "How AI Is Changing Your Job Hunt," *Fortune*, May 19, 2017. As of May 8, 2019:
http://fortune.com/2017/05/19/ai-changing-jobs-hiring-recruiting

American Academy of Actuaries, Committee on Risk Classification, *Risk Classification: Statement of Principles*, Washington, D.C.: American Academy of Actuaries Risk Classification Work Group, undated. As of May 8, 2019:
http://www.actuarialstandardsboard.org/wp-content/uploads/2014/07/riskclassificationSOP.pdf

American Academy of Actuaries, Risk Classification Work Group, *On Risk Classification*, Washington, D.C.: American Academy of Actuaries, 2011. As of May 1, 2019:
https://www.actuary.org/sites/default/files/files/publications/
RCWG_RiskMonograph_Nov2011.pdf

American Law Institute, *Model Penal Code: Sentencing*, proposed final draft, 2017. As of May 20, 2019:
https://robinainstitute.umn.edu/publications/
model-penal-code-sentencing-proposed-final-draft-approved-may-2017

Amnesty International and Access Now, "The Toronto Declaration: Protecting the Right to Equality and Non-Discrimination in Machine Learning Systems, May 16, 2018. As of May 10, 2019:
https://www.accessnow.org/cms/assets/uploads/2018/08/
The-Toronto-Declaration_ENG_08-2018.pdf

Amodei, Dario, Chris Olah, Jacob Steinhardt, Paul Christiano, John Schulman, and Dan Mané, "Concrete Problems in AI Safety," arXiv.org, 1606.06565, July 2016.

Anderson, Elizabeth, "What Is the Point of Equality?" *Ethics*, Vol. 109, No. 2, 1999, pp. 287–337.

Angwin, Julia, Jeff Larson, Surya Mattu and Lauren Kirchner, "Machine Bias," *ProPublica*, May 23, 2016. As of May 1, 2019:
https://www.propublica.org/article/machine-bias-risk-assessments-in-criminal-sentencing

———, "Minority Neighborhoods Pay Higher Car Insurance Premiums Than White Areas with the Same Risk," *ProPublica*, April 5, 2017. As of September 30, 2018:
https://www.propublica.org/article/
minority-neighborhoods-higher-car-insurance-premiums-white-areas-same-risk

Angwin, Julia, and Terry Parris, Jr., "Facebook Lets Advertisers Exclude Users by Race," *ProPublica*, October 28, 2016. As of May 8, 2019:
https://www.propublica.org/article/facebook-lets-advertisers-exclude-users-by-race

Angwin, Julia, Noam Scheiber, and Ariana Tobin, "Facebook Job Ads Raise Concerns About Age Discrimination," *New York Times*, December 20, 2017. As of May 8, 2019:
https://www.nytimes.com/2017/12/20/business/facebook-job-ads.html

Arnold, Thomas, Daniel Kasenberg, and Matthias Scheutz, "Value Alignment or Misalignment—What Will Keep Systems Accountable?" *AAAI Workshops 2017*, San Francisco: Association for the Advancement of Artificial Intelligence, February 2017.

Arrow, Kenneth J., *Social Choice and Individual Values*, 3rd edition, New Haven, Conn.: Yale University Press, 2012.

Avraham, Ronen, Kyle D. Logue, and Daniel Schwarcz, "Understanding Insurance Antidiscrimination Laws," *Southern California Law Review*, Vol. 87, No. 2, 2014a, pp. 195–274.

———, "Towards a Universal Framework for Insurance Anti-Discrimination Laws," *Connecticut Insurance Law Journal*, Vol. 21, No. 1, 2014b, pp. 1–52.

Barocas, Solon, and Andrew D. Selbst, "Big Data's Disparate Impact," *California Law Review*, Vol. 104, 2016.

Berk, Richard, Hoda Heidari, Shahin Jabbari, Matthew Joseph, Michael Kearns, Jamie Morgenstern, Seth Neel, and Aaron Roth, "A Convex Framework for Fair Regression," arXiv.org, 1706.02409, June 2017a.

Berk, Richard, Hoda Heidari, Shahin Jabbari, Michael Kearns, and Aaron Roth, "Fairness in Criminal Justice Risk Assessments: The State of the Art," arXiv.org, 1703.09207, May 2017b.

Berlin, Isaiah, "The Pursuit of the Ideal," in Isaiah Berlin, *The Proper Study of Mankind: An Anthology of Essays*, New York: Farrar, Straus, and Giroux, 2000.

Bertsimas, Dimitris, Vivek F. Farias, and Nikolaos Trichakis, "The Price of Fairness," *Operations Research*, Vol. 59, No. 1, 2011, pp. 17–31.

Biddle, "Uniform Employee Selection Guidelines on Employee Selection Procedures," webpage, undated. As of May 7, 2019:
http://www.uniformguidelines.com/uniformguidelines.html

Binns, Reuben, "What Can Political Philosophy Teach Us About Algorithmic Fairness?" *IEEE Security & Privacy*, Vol. 16, No. 3, 2018, pp. 73–80.

Borchard, Annegret, David L. B. Schwappach, Aline Barbir, and Paula Bezzola, "A Systematic Review of the Effectiveness, Compliance, and Critical Factors for Implementation of Safety Checklists in Surgery," *Annals of Surgery*, Vol. 256, No. 6, 2012, pp. 925–933.

Buolamwini, Joy, and Timnit Gebru, "Gender Shades: Intersectional Accuracy Disparities in Commercial Gender Classification," *Proceedings of Machine Learning Research*, Vol. 81, 2018, pp. 77–91.

Burgess, Ernest W., "Protecting the Public by Parole and by Parole Prediction," *Journal of Criminal Law and Criminology*, Vol. 27, No. 4, 1936.

Caers, Ralf, and Vanessa Castelyns, "LinkedIn and Facebook in Belgium: The Influences and Biases of Social Network Sites in Recruitment and Selection Procedures," *Social Science Computer Review*, Vol. 29, No. 4, 2011, pp. 437–448.

Calders, Toon, and Indrė Žliobaitė, "Why Unbiased Computational Processes Can Lead to Discriminative Decision Procedures," in Bart Custers, Toon Calders, Bart Schermer, and Tal Zarsky, eds., *Discrimination and Privacy in the Information Society*, Berlin: Springer, 2013, pp. 43–57.

California Civil Code, California Consumer Privacy Act, Sections 1798.100–198, 2018.

Carlson, Alyssa M., "The Need for Transparency in the Age of Predictive Sentencing Algorithms," *Iowa Law Review*, Vol. 103, 2017.

Chouldechova, Alexandra, "Fair Prediction with Disparate Impact: A Study of Bias in Recidivism Prediction Instruments," *Big Data*, Vol. 5, No. 2, 2017, pp. 153–163.

Cino, Jessica Gabel, "Deploying the Secret Police: The Use of Algorithms in the Criminal Justice System," *Georgia State University Law Review*, Vol. 34, 2018.

Cohen, Alma, and Peter Siegelman, "Testing for Adverse Selection in Insurance Markets," *Journal of Risk and Insurance*, Vol. 77, No. 1, 2010, pp. 39–84.

Cohen, G. A., "On the Currency of Egalitarian Justice," *Ethics*, Vol. 99, No. 4, July 1989, pp. 906–944.

Corbett-Davies, Sam, Emma Pierson, Avi Feller, Sharad Goel, and Aziz Huq, "Algorithmic Decision Making and the Cost of Fairness," *Proceedings of the 23rd Association for Computing Machinery's Special Interest Group on Knowledge Discovery and Data Mining International Conference on Knowledge Discovery and Data Mining*, Halifax, Canada: Association of Computing Machinery, August 2017, pp. 797–806.

Crawford, Kate, "The Trouble With Bias—NIPS 2017 Keynote—Kate Crawford," YouTube, 2017. As of May 8, 2019:
https://www.youtube.com/watch?v=fMym_BKWQzk

Cummings, M. L., "The Social and Ethical Impact of Decision Support Interface Design," in Waldemar Karwowski, ed., *International Encyclopedia of Ergonomics and Human Factors*, 2d ed., Boca Raton, Fl.: CRC Press, 2006.

Dastin, Jeffrey, "Amazon Scraps Secret AI Recruiting Tool that Showed Bias Against Women," Reuters, October 9, 2018. As of May 8, 2019:
https://www.reuters.com/article/us-amazon-com-jobs-automation-insight/
amazon-scraps-secret-ai-recruiting-tool-that-showed-bias-against-women-idUSKCN1MK08G

Desai, Deven R., and Joshua A. Kroll, "Trust but Verify: A Guide to Algorithms and the Law," *Harvard Journal of Law and Technology*, Vol. 31, No. 1, 2018.

Dickerson, John P., Ariel D. Procaccia, and Tuomas Sandholm, "Price of Fairness in Kidney Exchange," *Proceedings of the 2014 International Conference on Autonomous Agents and Multi-Agent Systems*, Paris: International Foundation for Autonomous Agents and Multiagent Systems, May 2014, pp. 1013–1020.

Dieterich, William, Christian Mendoza, and Tim Brennan, "COMPAS Risk Scales: Demonstrating Accuracy Equity and Predictive Parity," Northepointe Inc. Research Department, July 8, 2016. As of May 8, 2019:
http://go.volarisgroup.com/rs/430-MBX-989/images/ProPublica_Commentary_Final_070616.pdf

"Discrimination Through Artificial Intelligence Banned," *Daily Finland*, April 26, 2018. As of May 10, 2019:
http://www.dailyfinland.fi/national/5168/Discrimination-through-artificial-intelligence-banned

Dolan, Paul, Richard Edlin, Aki Tsuchiya, and Allan Wailoo, "It Ain't What You Do, It's the Way That You Do It: Characteristics of Procedural Justice and Their Importance in Social Decision-Making," *Journal of Economic Behavior and Organization*, Vol. 64, No. 1, 2007, pp. 157–170.

Dwork, Cynthia, Moritz Hardt, Toniann Pitassi, Omer Reingold, and Richard Zemel, "Fairness Through Awareness," *Proceedings of the 3rd Innovations in Theoretical Computer Science Conference*, Cambridge, Mass.: Association for Computing Machinery, January 2012, pp. 214–226.

Dworkin, Ronald, *Sovereign Virtue: The Theory and Practice of Equality*, Cambridge, Mass.: Harvard University Press, 2000.

EEOC—*See* U.S. Equal Employment Opportunity Commission.

Ensign, Danielle, Sorelle A. Friedler, Scott Neville, Carlos Scheidegger, and Suresh Venkatasubramanian, "Runaway Feedback Loops in Predictive Policing," *Proceedings of Machine Learning Research*, Vol. 81, 2018, pp. 1–12.

Entelo, "Opower Chooses Entelo and Increases Female Hires from 40% to 47% and Minority Technical Hires from 1.5% to 11%," press release, undated. As of May 8, 2019:
https://www.entelo.com/wp-content/uploads/2018/08/CS_Opower-6.25.18.pdf

———, "Entelo Reinvents the Candidate Profile with the Launch of Entelo Insights," press release, May 1, 2018. As of May 16, 2019:
https://www.entelo.com/press-releases/entelo-reinvents-the-candidate-profile-with-the-launch-of-entelo-insights

Eubanks, Virginia, *Automating Inequality: How High-Tech Tools Profile, Police, and Punish the Poor*, New York: St. Martin's Press, 2018.

Faliagka, Evanthia, Athanasios Tsakalidis, and Giannis Tzimas, "An Integrated E-Recruitment System for Automated Personality Mining and Applicant Ranking," *Internet Research*, Vol. 22, No. 5, 2012, pp. 551–568.

Fama, homepage, undated. As of May 8, 2019:
https://www.fama.io/#welcome

Feldman, Michael, Sorelle A. Friedler, John Moeller, Carlos Scheidegger, and Suresh Venkatasubramanian, "Certifying and Removing Disparate Impact," *Proceedings of the 21st Association for Computing Machinery's Special Interest Group on Knowledge Discovery and Data Mining International Conference on Knowledge Discovery and Data Mining*, Sydney, Australia: Association of Computing Machinery, August 2015, pp. 259–268.

Feloni, Richard, "Consumer-Goods Giant Unilever Has Been Hiring Employees Using Brain Games and Artificial Intelligence—And It's a Huge Success," *Business Insider*, June 28, 2017. As of May 8, 2019:
https://www.businessinsider.com/unilever-artificial-intelligence-hiring-process-2017-6

Fine Maron, Dina, "Science Career Ads Are Disproportionately Seen by Men," *Scientific American*, July 25, 2018. As of May 8, 2019:
https://www.scientificamerican.com/article/science-career-ads-are-disproportionately-seen-by-men

Fiscella, Kevin, and Allen M. Fremont, "Use of Geocoding and Surname Analysis to Estimate Race and Ethnicity," *Health Services Research*, Vol. 41, No. 4, Part 1, 2006, pp. 1482–1500.

Future of Life Institute, "Asilomar AI Principles," webpage, undated. As of May 10, 2019:
https://futureoflife.org/ai-principles

———, "State of California Endorses Asilomar AI Principles," webpage, August 31, 2018. As of May 10, 2019:
https://futureoflife.org/2018/08/31/state-of-california-endorses-asilomar-ai-principles

Ganchev, Kuzman, Michael Kearns, Yuriy Nevmyvaka, and Jennifer Wortman Vaughan, "Censored Exploration and the Dark Pool Problem," *Proceedings of the Twenty-Fifth Conference on Uncertainty in Artificial Intelligence*, Montreal: Association for Uncertainty in Artificial Intelligence, June 2009, pp. 185–194.

Gates, Susan Wharton, Vanessa Gail Perry, and Peter M. Zorn, "Automated Underwriting in Mortgage Lending: Good News for the Underserved?" *Housing Policy Debate*, Vol. 13, No. 2, 2002, pp. 369–391.

Gibbard, Allan, "Manipulation of Voting Schemes: A General Result," *Econometrica*, Vol. 41, No. 4, 1973, pp. 587–601.

Goldman, Rob, "This Time, ProPublica, We Disagree: Our View on Age-Based Targeting for Employment Ads," *Facebook Newsroom*, December 20, 2017. As of May 8, 2019:
https://newsroom.fb.com/news/h/addressing-targeting-in-recruitment-ads

Golle, Philippe, "Revisiting the Uniqueness of Simple Demographics in the US Population," *Proceedings of the 5th ACM Workshop on Privacy in Electronic Society*, Alexandria, Va.: Association for Computing Machinery, 2006, pp. 77–80.

Gottfredson, Don M., Leslie T. Wilkins, and Peter B. Hoffman, *Guidelines For Parole and Sentencing: A Policy Control Method*, Lexington, Mass.: Lexington Books, 1978.

Greenwood, Peter W., and Allan Abrahamse, *Selective Incapacitation*, Santa Monica, Calif.: RAND Corporation, R-2815-NIJ, 1982. As of May 9, 2019:
https://www.rand.org/pubs/reports/R2815.html

Griggs v. Duke Power Co., 401 U.S. 424, 91 S. Ct. 849, 1971.

Hadfield-Menell, Dylan, Stuart J. Russell, Pieter Abbeel, and Anca Dragan, "Cooperative Inverse Reinforcement Learning," *Advances in Neural Information Processing Systems*, Vol. 29, 2016, pp. 3909–3917.

Hamilton, Melissa, "Risk-Needs Assessment: Constitutional and Ethical Challenges," *American Criminal Law Review*, Vol. 52, 2015.

Hardt, Moritz, Eric Price, and Nathan Srebro, "Equality of Opportunity in Supervised Learning," *Advances in Neural Information Processing Systems*, Vol. 29, 2016, pp. 3315–3323.

Hoffman, Peter B., "Screening for Risk: A Revisited Salient Factor Score (SFS 81)," *Journal of Criminal Justice*, Vol. 11, No. 6, December 1983, pp. 539–547.

Ideal, "Customers: Indigo, North America's Books & Music Destination," webpage, undated. As of May 8, 2019:
https://ideal.com/customer/indigo-books-music

Institute of Electrical and Electronics Engineers, *Ethically Aligned Design: A Vision for Prioritizing Human Well-Being with Autonomous and Intelligent Systems*, Version 2, Piscataway, N.J., undated. As of May 10, 2019:
https://standards.ieee.org/content/dam/ieee-standards/standards/web/documents/other/ead_v2.pdf

Keats Citron, Danielle, "Technological Due Process," *Washington University Law Review*, Vol. 85, No. 6, 2008.

Keats Citron, Danielle, and Frank Pasquale, "The Scored Society: Due Process for Automated Predictions," *Washington Law Review*, Vol. 89, No. 1, 2014.

Kehl, Danielle, Priscilla Guo, and Samuel Kessler, *Algorithms in the Criminal Justice System: Assessing the Use of Risk Assessments in Sentencing*, Cambridge, Mass.: Responsive Communities Initiative, Berkman Klein Center for Internet & Society, Harvard Law School, 2017. As of May 20, 2019: http://nrs.harvard.edu/urn-3:HUL.InstRepos:33746041

Kleinberg, Jon, Jens Ludwig, Sendhil Mullainathan, and Ashesh Rambachan, "Algorithmic Fairness," *AEA Papers and Proceedings*, Vol. 108, 2018, pp. 22–27.

Kleinberg, Jon, Sendhil Mullainathan, and Manish Raghavan, "Inherent Trade-Offs in the Fair Determination of Risk Scores," arXiv.org, 1609.05807, November 2016.

Kusner, Matt J., Joshua Loftus, Chris Russell, and Ricardo Silva, "Counterfactual Fairness," *Advances in Neural Information Processing Systems*, Vol. 30, 2017, pp. 4066–4076.

Lansing, Sharon, *New York State COMPAS-Probation Risk and Need Assessment Study: Examining the Recidivism Scale's Effectiveness and Predictive Accuracy*, Albany, N.Y.: Division of Criminal Justice Services Office of Justice Research and Performance, September 2012. As of May 8, 2019: http://www.northpointeinc.com/downloads/research/ DCJS_OPCA_COMPAS_Probation_Validity.pdf

Levendowski, Amanda, "How Copyright Law Can Fix Artificial Intelligence's Implicit Bias Problem," *Washington Law Review*, Vol. 93, 2018.

Locke, John, *Two Treatises of Government*, 1689.

Marchant, Gary, and Wendell Wallach, "Coordinating Technology Governance," *Issues in Science and Technology*, Vol. 31, No. 4, Summer 2015.

Markham, Jamie, "Probation's Risk-Needs Assessment in a Nutshell," *North Carolina Criminal Law Blog*, August 8, 2012. As of August 9, 2018: http://nccriminallaw.sog.unc.edu/wp-content/uploads/2012/08/RNA-process-in-a-nutshell.pdf

Maurer, Roy, "Screening Candidates' Social Media May Lead to TMI, Discrimination Claims," *SHRM*, April 23, 2018. As of May 8, 2019: https://www.shrm.org/resourcesandtools/hr-topics/talent-acquisition/pages/ screening-social-media-discrimination-claims.aspx

Mcdonnell Douglas Corp. v. Green, 411 U.S. 792, 93 S. Ct. 1817, 1973.

Microsoft, "Microsoft's Commitment to GDPR, Privacy and Putting Customers in Control of Their Own Data," blog post, May 21, 2018. As of May 20, 2019: https://blogs.microsoft.com/on-the-issues/2018/05/21/ microsofts-commitment-to-gdpr-privacy-and-putting-customers-in-control-of-their-own-data

Mitchell, Margaret, Simone Wu, Andrew Zaldivar, Parker Barnes, Lucy Vasserman, Ben Hutchinson, Elena Spitzer, Inioluwa Deborah Raji, and Timnit Gebru, "Model Cards for Model Reporting," arxiv.org, 1810.03993, January 2019.

Monahan, John, and Jennifer L. Skeem, "Risk Redux: The Resurgence of Risk Assessment in Criminal Sanctioning," *Federal Sentencing Reporter*, Vol. 26, No. 3, 2014, pp. 158–166.

Moulin, Hervé, *Fair Division and Collective Welfare*, Cambridge, Mass.: MIT Press, 2004.

National Association of Insurance Commissioners, "Casualty Actuarial and Statistical (C) Task Force Price: Optimization White Paper," Kansas City, Mo., November 19, 2015. As of May 8, 2019: https://www.naic.org/documents/committees_c_catf_related_price_optimization_white_paper.pdf

National Commission for the Protection of Human Subjects of Biomedical and Behavioral Research, *The Belmont Report: Ethical Principles and Guidelines for the Protection of Human Subjects of Research*, Bethesda, Md., April 18, 1979. As of May 1, 2019:
https://www.hhs.gov/ohrp/regulations-and-policy/belmont-report/read-the-belmont-report/index.html

Nilsson, Nils J., *Artificial Intelligence: A New Synthesis*, Amsterdam: Elsevier, 1998.

North Carolina Department of Public Safety, Division of Adult Correction and Juvenile Justice, Community Corrections, *Policy and Procedures,* Raleigh, N.C., August 1, 2016. As of May 16, 2019:
https://ncdps.s3.amazonaws.com/s3fs-public/documents/files/Policy_0.pdf

———, *Report on Probation and Parole Caseloads*, March 1, 2018. As of August 9, 2018:
https://www.ncleg.net/documentsites/committees/JLOCJPS/Reports/FY%202017-18/DPS_Report_on_Probation_and_Parole_Caseloads_2018_03_01.pdf

Nozick, Robert, *Anarchy, State, and Utopia*, New York: Basic Books, 1974.

O'Leary, Daniel, "Exploiting Big Data from Mobile Device Sensor-Based Apps: Challenges and Benefits," *MIS Quarterly Executive*, Vol. 12, No. 4, December 2013, pp. 179–187.

Ong, Paul M., and Michael A. Stoll, "Redlining or Risk? A Spatial Analysis of Auto Insurance Rates in Los Angeles," *Journal of Policy Analysis and Management*, Vol. 26, No. 4, 2007, pp. 811–830.

Organization for Economic Cooperation and Development, "OECD Data: Insurance Spending," webpage, 2018. As of May 8, 2019:
https://data.oecd.org/insurance/insurance-spending.htm

Osoba, Osonde A., and William Welser, IV, *An Intelligence in Our Image: The Risks of Bias and Errors in Artificial Intelligence*, Santa Monica, Calif.: RAND Corporation, RR-1744-RC, 2017a. As of May 1, 2019:
https://www.rand.org/pubs/research_reports/RR1744.html

———, *The Risks of Artificial Intelligence to Security and the Future of Work*, Santa Monica, Calif.: RAND Corporation, 2017b. As of May 1, 2019:
https://www.rand.org/pubs/perspectives/PE237.html

Ostrom, Brian J., Matthew Kleiman, Fred Cheesman, II, Randall M. Hansen, and Neal B. Kauder, *Offender Risk Assessment in Virginia: A Three-Stage Evaluation: Process of Sentencing Reform, Empirical Study of Diversion and Recidivism, Benefit-Cost Analysis*, National Center for State Courts and the Virginia Criminal Sentencing Commission, 2002. As of May 20, 2019:
http://www.vcsc.virginia.gov/risk_off_rpt.pdf

Pager, Devah, and David S. Pedulla, "Race, Self-Selection, and the Job Search Process," *American Journal of Sociology*, Vol. 120, No. 4, 2015, pp. 1005–1054.

Podesta, John, "Big Data: Values and Governance," remarks delivered at the UC Berkeley School of Information, Berkeley Center for Law and Technology Workshop, Berkeley, Calif., April 1, 2014. As of June 26, 2019:
https://obamawhitehouse.archives.gov/sites/default/files/docs/040114_remarks_john_podesta_big_data_1.pdf

Raiffa, Howard, and Robert Schlaifer, *Applied Statistical Decision Theory*, Boston: Harvard University, 1961.

Rawls, John, *A Theory of Justice*, rev. ed., Cambridge, Mass.: Harvard University Press, 2009.

Regulation (EU) 2016/679 of the European Parliament and of the Council of 27 April 2016 on the Protection of Natural Persons with Regard to the Processing of Personal Data and on the Free Movement of Such Data, and Repealing Directive 95/46/EC, *Official Journal of the European Union*, Vol. L119, May 4, 2016, pp. 1–88.

Reisman, Dillon, Jason Schultz, Kate Crawford, and Meredith Whittaker, *Algorithmic Impact Assessments: A Practical Framework for Public Agency Accountability*, New York: AI Now Institute at New York University, April 2018. As of May 16, 2019: https://ainowinstitute.org/aiareport2018.pdf

Ricci v. Destefano, 557 U.S. 557, 129 S. Ct. 2658, 2009.

Ruths, Derek, and Jürgen Pfeffer, "Social Media for Large Studies of Behavior," *Science*, Vol. 346, No. 6213, 2014, pp. 1063–1064.

Scheffler, Samuel, *Equality and Tradition Questions of Value in Moral and Political Theory*, New York: Oxford University Press, 2012.

Sen, Amartya, *Collective Choice and Social Welfare: An Expanded Edition*, Cambridge, Mass.: Harvard University Press, 2018.

Simmons, Ric, "Big Data and Procedural Justice: Legitimizing Algorithms in the Criminal Justice System," *Ohio State Journal of Criminal Law*, Vol. 15, No. 2, 2018, pp. 573–581.

Singh, Amit, Catherine Rose, Karthik Visweswariah, and Vijil Chenthamarakshan, "PROSPECT: A System for Screening Candidates for Recruitment," Toronto: *Proceedings of the 19th Association for Computing Machinery International Conference on Information and Knowledge Management,* October 2010, pp. 659–668.

Skeem, Jennifer, and John Monahan, "Current Directions in Violence Risk Assessment*,"* *Current Directions in Psychological Science*, Vol. 20, No. 1, 2011, pp. 38–42.

Skitka, Linda J., Kathleen L. Mosier, Mark Burdick, and Bonnie Rosenblatt, "Automation Bias and Errors: Are Crews Better Than Individuals?" *International Journal of Aviation Psychology*, Vol. 10, 2000, pp. 85–97.

Soares, Nate, and Benja Fallenstein, *Aligning Superintelligence with Human Interests: A Technical Research Agenda*, Berkeley, Calif.: Machine Intelligence Research Institute, 2014. As of May 7, 2019: https://pdfs.semanticscholar.org/b9a2/a32bbfb6530e61db4710f1c3028004e5f298.pdf

Spice, Byron, "Questioning the Fairness of Targeting Ads Online," *Carnegie Mellon University*, July 7, 2015. As of May 8, 2019: https://www.cmu.edu/news/stories/archives/2015/july/online-ads-research.html

Squires, Gregory D., "Why an Insurance Regulation to Prohibit Redlining?" *John Marshall Law Review*, Vol. 31, 1998.

State v. Loomis, 881 N.W.2d 749, 766 Wisconsin, 2016.

Storm, Darlene, "Google Concerned About Curious but Destructive Cleaning Robots that Hack Reward Systems," *Computerworld*, June 22, 2016. As of May 7, 2019: https://www.computerworld.com/article/3087328/google-concerned-about-curious-but-destructive-cleaning-robots-that-hack-reward-systems.html

Sweeney, Latanya, *Simple Demographics Often Identify People Uniquely*, Pittsburgh: Carnegie Mellon University, Data Privacy Working Paper 3, 2000. As of May 7, 2019: https://dataprivacylab.org/projects/identifiability/paper1.pdf

Sweeney, Latanya, "Discrimination in Online Ad Delivery," arXiv.org, 1301.6822, January 2013.

Taigman, Yaniv, Ming Yang, Marc'Aurelio Ranzato, and Lior Wolf, "Deepface: Closing the Gap to Human-Level Performance in Face Verification," *Proceedings of the IEEE Conference on Computer Vision and Pattern Recognition*, Columbus, Ohio: Institute of Electrical and Electronics Engineers, June 2014, pp. 1701–1708.

Talvista, "How We Do It," webpage, undated. As of May 8, 2019:
https://www.talvista.com/#howwedoit

Textio, "Textio Hire," webpage, undated. As of May 8, 2019:
https://textio.com/products/

Tonry, Michael, "Sentencing in America: 1975–2025," *Crime and Justice*, Vol. 42, No. 1, August 2013, pp. 141–198.

———, "Legal and Ethical Issues in the Prediction of Recidivism," *Federal Sentencing Reporter*, Vol. 26, 2014.

Truxillo, Donald M., Talya N. Bauer, and Rudolph J. Sanchez, "Multiple Dimensions of Procedural Justice: Longitudinal Effects on Selection System Fairness and Test-Taking Self-Efficacy," *International Journal of Selection and Assessment*, Vol. 9, No. 4, December 2001, pp. 336–349.

Tyler, Tom R., "Psychological Models of the Justice Motive: Antecedents of Distributive and Procedural Justice," *Journal of Personality and Social Psychology*, Vol. 67, No. 5, 1994, pp. 850–863.

———, "Procedural Justice, Legitimacy, and the Effective Rule of Law," *Crime and Justice*, Vol. 30, 2003, pp. 283–357.

U.S. Equal Employment Opportunity Commission, "Discrimination by Type," webpage, undated. As of May 8, 2019:
https://www.eeoc.gov/laws/types/index.cfm

Utah Sentencing Commission, "Adult Sentencing and Release Determinations: Philosophical Approach," June 2012. As of June 26, 2019:
https://justice.utah.gov/Sentencing/Policy/Philosophical%20Statement.pdf

Vallor, Shannon, Brian Green, and Irina Raicu, "Overview of Ethics in Tech Practice," Markkula Center for Applied Ethics at Santa Clara University, June 22, 2018. As of May 1, 2019:
https://www.scu.edu/ethics-in-technology-practice/overview-of-ethics-in-tech-practice

Washington State Office of the Attorney General, "AG Ferguson Investigation Leads to Facebook Making Nationwide Changes to Prohibit Discriminatory Advertisements on Its Platform," press release, July 24, 2018. As of May 8, 2019:
https://www.atg.wa.gov/news/news-releases/
ag-ferguson-investigation-leads-facebook-making-nationwide-changes-prohibit

Walzer, Michael, *Spheres of Justice: A Defense of Pluralism and Equality*, New York: Basic Books, 1983.

Wexler, Rebecca, "Life, Liberty, and Trade Secrets: Intellectual Property in the Criminal Justice System," *Stanford Law Review,* Vol. 70, 2018.

Wroblewski, Jonathan, letter to Patti B. Saris, Washington, D.C., dated July 29, 2014. As of May 9, 2019:
https://www.justice.gov/sites/default/files/criminal/legacy/2014/08/01/
2014annual-letter-final-072814.pdf

Young, H. Peyton, *Equity: In Theory and Practice*, Princeton, N.J.: Princeton University Press, 1995.

Zant v. Stephens, 462 U.S. 862, 874, 1983.

About the Authors

Osonde A. Osoba is an information scientist at the RAND Corporation. He applies machine learning models to problems in diverse policy domains and examines the policy implications of artificial intelligence. Osoba has a Ph.D. in electrical engineering.

Benjamin Boudreaux is a policy researcher at the RAND Corporation. His research focuses on policy issues at the intersection of national security, technology, and ethics. He has a Ph.D. in philosophy.

Jessica Saunders is an adjunct policy researcher at the RAND Corporation. She has fifteen years of experience conducting applied research with criminal justice systems agencies on such topics as community crime prevention, policing, corrections, and re-entry. Saunders has a Ph.D. in criminal justice.

J. Luke Irwin is an assistant policy researcher at the RAND Corporation and a doctoral candidate at the Pardee RAND Graduate School. His primary interests are in emerging technologies and the implications of automation for the future of work. Irwin has an M.P.H.

Pam A. Mueller is a social psychologist and a lawyer. Her research has primarily used experimental methodologies to explore issues in civil and criminal law. She has a J.D. and a Ph.D. in social psychology.

Samantha Cherney is a quantitative analyst at the RAND Corporation. She has worked on a wide variety of projects at RAND, with a focus on legal and regulatory issues. She has a J.D.